HEALTH REPORTS:
DISEASES AND DISORDERS

ALLERGIES

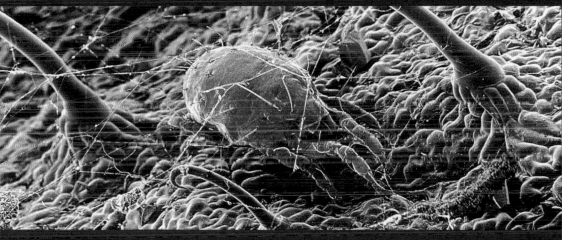

WENDY MORAGNE

To my husband, Perry, and my daughter Gailynn, whose allergies have changed our lives, and to my daughter Brynn, the diligent food-label reader, who so lovingly protects her little sister

Twenty-First Century Books
A division of Lerner Publishing Group, Inc.
241 First Avenue North
Minneapolis, MN 55401 U.S.A.

Website address: www.lernerbooks.com

Library of Congress Cataloging-in-Publication Data

Moragne, Wendy.
    Allergies / by Wendy Moragne.
        p.   cm. — (USA today health reports: Diseases and disorders)
        Includes bibliographical references and index.
        ISBN 978–0–7613–6089–6 (lib. bdg. : alk. paper)
        1. Allergy—Juvenile literature. I. Title.
    RC585.M673 2012
    616.97—dc22   2011001253

Manufactured in the United States of America
1 – MG – 7/15/11

CONTENTS

USA TODAY
HEALTH REPORTS:
DISEASES AND DISORDERS

CHAPTER ONE

WHAT ARE ALLERGIES?

The search for relief of allergy symptoms sends more people to the doctor than any other medical condition. An estimated 55 percent of Americans have allergies. Some sniffle and sneeze their way through life without much interruption. Others feel so miserable that their symptoms interfere with school, work, or just having a good time. And for some, the symptoms can be life threatening.

If one or both of your parents have allergies, there is a strong likelihood that you will develop them as well. You inherit the tendency to develop an allergy, but you may not necessarily be allergic to the same substance. If your mother is allergic to eggs and your father is allergic to pollen, you may end up being allergic to bee venom.

Allergic reactions involve the immune system. Think of your immune system as an army of defense cells. Then think of bacteria, viruses, fungi, and parasitic worms as enemies. When the body is invaded by one of these things, the immune system gears up to protect it from disease. The immune systems of people with allergies react in the same way to allergens, which are substances that cause allergic reactions. The immune systems of these people are hypersensitive, or overly sensitive. They mistake harmless substances (such as eggs or pollen) for harmful organisms (such as bacteria or parasitic worms). Something in the genetic makeup of the body signals the immune system to react this way.

In people with allergies, the immune system fights harmless substances just as hard as it fights harmful substances. In someone who is allergic to eggs, for example, the immune system fights as hard against a bite of hard-boiled egg as it would against a bite of undercooked pork infested with trichinae. These parasitic worms have larvae that live in the intestines and muscles of humans and cause a serious disease called trichinosis.

Do You Have Allergies?

Have you ever wondered whether you have allergies? Here is a quiz that can help you find out if you do. If you answer yes to any of these questions, you might have allergies. The way to find out for sure is to see a doctor.

- Do you feel as if you always have a cold?

- Does mucus constantly drip down your throat?

- Do you clear your throat a lot?

- Do you have a constant cough?

- Do your eyes itch and water?

- Do you have dark rings or swelling around your eyes?

- Do your ears feel full or do they pop?

- Do your sinuses frequently become congested?

- Do you suffer from itchy skin rashes?

- Do you wheeze when you breathe?

- Do you have difficulty breathing at night?

- Do you often have abdominal cramps, nausea, diarrhea, or bloating?

- Do you have frequent headaches?

- Do you feel tired and irritable much of the time?

Allergies usually begin to develop in childhood, although they can appear at any age. Generally, for people who have the tendency to develop allergies, the more often and the more directly they come in contact with an allergen, the more likely they are to develop an allergy to it. For example, if you have inherited the tendency to develop an allergy and you have a cat, you might develop an allergy to cat dander. These tiny dandrufflike scales shed from animal skin, feathers, or hair. Because you are exposed to the cat's dander every day at home, you are likely to become allergic to it.

SUBSTANCES THAT CAUSE ALLERGIC REACTIONS

People with allergies react to substances they encounter every day. Allergens are in the air, in our food, and in things we touch. They are breathed in, ingested (eaten), injected into the skin, or touched. And it is possible to be allergic to more than one allergen.

Allergens we breathe in include:
- pollens
- mold spores
- dust
- decaying dust mites and their droppings
- decaying cockroaches and their droppings
- dander, saliva, and urine of animals and birds

Allergens that enter the body through the mouth include:
- food, especially eggs, milk, tree nuts, peanuts, and seafood
- drugs taken by mouth, especially penicillin and sulfa drugs (used to treat bacterial infections)

This honey bee collects nectar from a flower. Many stinging insects inject venom into their victims. People can develop allergies to insect venom.

Injected and ingested allergens include:
- insect venom, especially from bees, bumblebees, wasps, yellow jackets, hornets, and fire ants
- injected drugs, especially penicillin

Allergens that are touched include:
- latex rubber
- certain metals
- cosmetics

SYMPTOMS OF AN ALLERGIC REACTION

Symptoms of an allergic reaction can be so mild that they are hardly noticeable or so severe that they can cause death. They may be seasonal, or they may occur throughout the year. Allergic symptoms sometimes

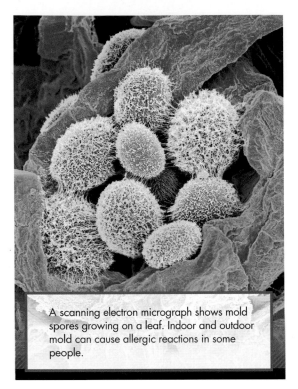

A scanning electron micrograph shows mold spores growing on a leaf. Indoor and outdoor mold can cause allergic reactions in some people.

lessen gradually with age, and some disappear completely. But often they reappear later in life.

The symptoms of an allergic reaction depend on the allergen. The inhaled allergens (those that are breathed)—pollens, mold spores, dust and dust mites, cockroach droppings, and animal dander—affect the respiratory system and cause sneezing, a stuffy and runny nose, and watery eyes.

Ingested (those that are eaten) and injected allergens—foods, drugs, and insect venom—can cause a reaction on or in almost any part of the body. Symptoms can range from sneezing, itching, and hives to nausea, vomiting, and diarrhea. Symptoms sometimes can escalate to anaphylaxis. This extreme allergic reaction can include a drop in blood pressure, loss of consciousness, and even death.

Allergens that affect the skin usually cause a rash. But some, such as latex rubber, can cause anaphylaxis and even death.

THE ROLE OF THE IMMUNE SYSTEM IN AN ALLERGIC REACTION

To understand what happens during an allergic reaction, we first must examine how the immune system works. The immune system

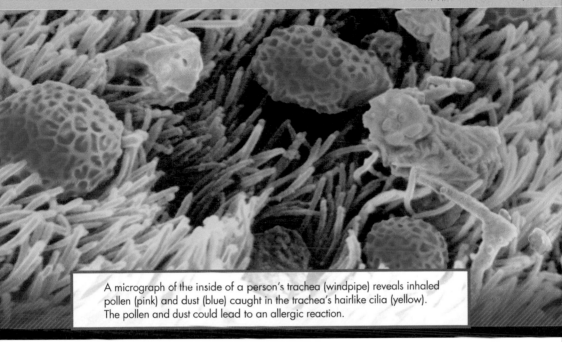

A micrograph of the inside of a person's trachea (windpipe) reveals inhaled pollen (pink) and dust (blue) caught in the trachea's hairlike cilia (yellow). The pollen and dust could lead to an allergic reaction.

is a complex network of specialized cells and organs that searches for, recognizes, and destroys enemy invaders of the body. In people who have allergies, the immune system considers allergens enemy invaders in the same way it considers germs enemy invaders.

Lymphocytes, antibodies, eosinophils, basophils, mast cells, and chemical mediators form the immune system's army in the battle against allergens. Each plays a specific role, and they work together to cause an allergic reaction.

Lymphocytes are the top-ranking soldiers of the immune system. These white blood cells are produced in the bone marrow—the tissue in the center of bones that manufactures all blood cells. One type of lymphocyte, the B lymphocyte, is the one called upon to fight the allergy battle. When an allergen invades the body, B lymphocytes are stimulated to mature and become a new kind of cell, called a plasma cell. Plasma cells produce antibodies and release them into the blood.

Antibodies, also called immunoglobulins, are special types of proteins that B lymphocytes produce to fight infections or allergens.

There are five types of antibodies—IgE, IgM, IgA, IgD, and IgG. Immunoglobulin E, or IgE, is the antibody involved in most allergic reactions. Each allergen stimulates production of its own specific IgE antibody. An IgE antibody produced to respond to ragweed pollen, for example, will react against only ragweed pollen and not birch tree pollen or any other kind of pollen.

Eosinophils are white blood cells that normally battle large enemy invaders such as parasitic worms, but they also respond when allergens enter the body. Doctors can see eosinophils under a microscope in nasal and bronchial mucus from hay fever and asthma sufferers. Because of this, doctors often call these cells allergy cells.

Basophils are white blood cells that contain chemical mediators released during an allergic reaction. IgE antibodies attach to basophils and cover their outer surfaces.

Mast cells line the respiratory tract, gastrointestinal tract, and skin. Like basophils, they produce and store chemical mediators and release these chemicals during an allergic reaction. IgE antibodies cover the outer surfaces of mast cells too.

Chemical mediators are chemical substances found in our bodies. Histamine is chief among them. In someone who is allergic, when an allergen enters the body, it attaches to IgE antibodies. Then mast cells and basophils release histamine and other chemical mediators as the immune system attempts to fight off the allergen and protect the body. Chemical mediators circulate through the body and cause the symptoms associated with allergic reactions. They cause muscle tightening, expansion of blood vessels, leakage of fluid from these blood vessels, and production of extra mucus. This leads to the development of symptoms in various parts of the body. For example, chemical mediators released in the sinuses, nose, and eyes cause sneezing, a runny nose, and itchy eyes. Those released in the lungs cause narrowing and swelling of the lining of the airways and the production of thick mucus. Those released in the digestive system cause stomach cramps and diarrhea. And those released in the skin cause rashes and hives.

HOW AN ALLERGIC REACTION DEVELOPS

An allergic reaction cannot take place until there is sensitization. Sensitization is the process of developing an allergy. This process begins the first time a person is exposed to the allergen. A period of days, weeks, months, or even years may pass before the process is complete and symptoms appear. Symptoms may appear on the second exposure or not until the hundredth exposure. Once the sensitization process is complete, even a tiny amount of the allergen can cause symptoms to develop.

An allergic reaction occurs soon after exposure to an allergen. Symptoms may appear seconds, minutes, or hours (usually no more than four) after exposure. When you have an allergic reaction, the allergen enters your body, stimulating the B lymphocytes to mature and become plasma cells. The plasma cells begin producing IgE antibodies specific to the allergen. If the allergen is mold, for example, then IgE antibodies specific to mold are produced. The IgE antibodies attach to the surrounding mast cells and basophils, covering their surfaces. Once this is complete, a person is sensitized to the allergen and is allergic to it. In this example, the person is allergic to mold and will have a reaction each time the body comes in contact with it. The mold spores enter the body and immediately attach to the IgE antibodies on the surfaces of the mast cells and basophils. The mold allergen is an exact fit with the IgE antibodies because the IgE antibodies the body produced during sensitization are specific for mold only.

Think of the fit as a car lock and key—only one key fits the lock and starts the engine. In the same way, the mold spores fit the IgE antibodies exactly and turn on, or activate, the mast cells and basophils.

www.usatoday.com

News
SECTION A

August 8, 2005

From the Pages of USA TODAY

Allergy sensitivity doubles since 1970s; Researchers unsure what's behind increase

More than half of all Americans test positive in response to one or more allergens, double the percentage who did 30 years ago, a new study reports.

Researchers at the National Institutes of Health found that 54% of people tested positive to at least one of 10 allergens. The highest response was to dust mites *(below)*, 27.5%. The lowest was to peanuts, 8.6%. The findings appear in the August issue of the *Journal of Allergy and Clinical Immunology*.

Researchers analyzed data from skin-prick allergy tests on 10,500 people by the Centers for Disease Control and Prevention.

The number of positive reactions is much higher than cases of actual allergic disease, notes lead researcher Samuel Arbes of the National Institutes of Health. A positive skin test for allergens such as ragweed or cats doesn't necessarily mean a person has or will develop allergies, but there is a strong association between the two.

About 20% of U.S. residents have allergies or hay fever; 8% to 10% have asthma.

Though there is evidence asthma rates have peaked, allergy rates appear to still be increasing, Arbes says.

Researchers don't know why positive skin tests, allergy and asthma are increasing. One theory is that people simply don't go outside as often and have higher exposures to indoor allergens. Another theory is that children have less resistance now because they are exposed to fewer bacteria and viruses.

—*Elizabeth Weise*

Once activated, the mast cells and basophils release histamine and other chemical mediators into the surrounding tissue. Then symptoms of the allergic reaction appear. You would begin to sneeze, your nose would become stuffy and runny, and your eyes would water and itch. The amount of IgE in your body determines how much histamine and other chemical mediators the immune system releases. The amount of chemicals released affects the severity of the reaction.

WHERE SYMPTOMS APPEAR

In an allergic reaction to latex rubber, the symptoms may appear just in the place where the allergen contacted the body. For example, if you wear a swimsuit made with spandex, which contains latex, you may break out in a rash only on the part of

Medical professionals commonly use disposable latex gloves to help prevent the spread of germs and other contaminants from patient to patient. Non-latex gloves are used more often to avoid harming people who are allergic to latex.

your body that the swimsuit covers. But in more severe reactions to latex, and in reactions to other allergens, symptoms sometimes appear in areas separate from the point of contact. This is because allergens travel.

Allergens can enter the body in one area, get into the bloodstream, and travel to other parts of the body. If you eat a food to which you are allergic, for example, the food enters your body through the mouth, and you digest it. It then enters the bloodstream from which it can travel to the skin and activate mast cells. The activated mast cells in the skin release histamine and other chemicals, causing a rash or hives.

Some reactions are even more widespread and involve many areas of the body. Symptoms may include a stuffy and runny nose, watery eyes, stomach cramps, diarrhea, nausea, vomiting, hives, and skin rash. For instance, an allergic reaction to food may cause swollen lips, upset stomach, congested nose, and hives. Occasionally, a reaction escalates to anaphylaxis, the most severe of all allergic reactions.

ANAPHYLAXIS

Anaphylaxis can be triggered by a number of allergens. The reaction is immediate, appearing within seconds to a few minutes after exposure to a substance. It may begin with itching around the eyes, widespread hives, a cough, and a feeling of anxiety. The episode may worsen amazingly quickly. The chest may tighten and cause wheezing. The throat may begin to close. Nausea, dizziness, and confusion may set in, followed by a sense of enveloping doom. All of this can happen from a single bee sting, an injection of penicillin, or a bite of food. Even putting on a swimsuit can be dangerous to someone with a latex allergy. And unfortunately, doctors cannot predict who will have an anaphylactic reaction to an allergen and who will not.

Some substances known to cause anaphylaxis include:

- drugs such as penicillin and insulin
- foods such as milk, eggs, fish and shellfish, tree nuts, peanuts, and seeds (such as sesame seeds)
- insect venom from bees, wasps, yellow jackets, hornets, and fire ants
- latex rubber in rubber gloves, adhesive bandages, condoms, and some clothing and sports equipment

Anaphylaxis can occur only after an individual is sensitized to the allergen. The individual must have encountered the allergen prior to the anaphylactic reaction. For example, someone may have been stung by a bee as a child and developed a small, red bump on the skin. Then, as an adult, when stung again, the reaction involves swelling of the throat, a sharp drop in blood pressure, and loss of consciousness. After the first sting, the body made antibodies to the bee venom and became sensitized. Then, years later, the body overreacted to the venom in the second sting.

Severe swelling of this boy's upper lip happened after he was stung by a hornet. If his body becomes sensitized to the antibodies in hornet venom, a future reaction could be much more severe.

Several body organs are involved during anaphylaxis. The following are the most frequent symptoms that occur in each of the four major organ systems:

SKIN

- hives or flush
- itching
- pale skin (due to drop in blood pressure)
- blue skin (due to swelling of the throat and lack of oxygen in the lungs)

DIGESTIVE TRACT

- stomach pain
- diarrhea
- nausea
- vomiting

HEART AND BLOOD VESSELS

- sharply increased or slowed heart rate
- chest pain or tightness
- drop in blood pressure

BRONCHIAL AND RESPIRATORY SYSTEM

- wheezing
- coughing
- swelling of the throat
- severe shortness of breath

Anaphylaxis can be life threatening. It requires immediate emergency medical treatment. An injection of the drug epinephrine can reverse the reaction if given immediately after the reaction

In the case of an anaphylactic reaction, a person would receive a shot from an EpiPen. The EpiPen delivers a quick shot of epinephrine, which helps treat the symptoms of a severe allergic reaction, giving the patient time to get to the emergency room.

begins. The patient should be in the emergency room of the hospital within five to fifteen minutes of the onset of the reaction.

If a person has had an anaphylactic reaction to a certain allergen, it is likely that a similar reaction will occur if exposed to that allergen again. If you have had an anaphylactic reaction to a bee sting, for example, you are likely to have an anaphylactic reaction the next time you are stung. People at risk should carry injectable epinephrine to use at the first sign of an allergic reaction so they will have time to get to the hospital. Injectable epinephrine, such as the EpiPen, is available by prescription from a doctor.

Anyone who has ever had an anaphylactic reaction should wear a medical emergency tag, such as a bracelet or a necklace available through MedicAlert. The tag lists the substances to which the person is allergic. That way, emergency medical personnel and doctors are aware of what has triggered the reaction, such as bee venom, or what will trigger a reaction, such as penicillin.

CHAPTER TWO

DIAGNOSIS AND TREATMENT

The first step in treating allergies is finding their cause. This is not always easy. If you sneeze and cough every time you pet your friend's dog, obviously, dog dander causes a reaction. But if you react with hives and stomach cramps after you eat a meal, it can be difficult to determine which ingredient in the meal caused the reaction. Many family doctors will refer their patients to a specialist, called an allergist, for help with diagnosing allergies.

PATIENT HISTORY

In making a diagnosis, the doctor will begin by gathering some important information about you. This is called a patient history. The doctor will ask questions like the following:

- What are the exact symptoms you experience?
- Are the symptoms the same every time you have a reaction?
- Do your symptoms appear only at certain times of the year?
- Do your symptoms appear only on certain days of the week, such as school days or weekends?
- If you have a part-time job, do your symptoms appear only when you are at work?
- Do you have any pets?
- What types of pillow, mattress, and blanket do you use, and how long have you had them?
- How is your home heated and cooled?
- Have you treated your symptoms with medications? If so, have they helped?
- Do you take other medications, such as those for pain relief?
- Do other people in your family have allergies?

PHYSICAL EXAMINATION

The next step is a thorough physical examination. The doctor will check your heart, lungs, eyes, ears, nose, nervous reflexes, and muscle tone. The doctor will also look for signs of allergy, such as hives or rashes, patches of red skin, watery eyes, an inflamed throat, and a purplish lining of the nose. Other conditions resemble allergies, so the doctor will have to rule these out before making a diagnosis. Laboratory tests and X-rays often help doctors diagnose allergies.

TESTS FOR ALLERGIES

Once the doctor suspects allergy, based on what he or she discovers from the patient history and the physical examination, tests can help confirm the diagnosis. For an accurate diagnosis, the doctor must consider all the information gathered through the patient history, physical examination, and test results.

After talking with patients and running a variety of tests, doctors can determine the cause of allergic reactions and recommend treatment and prevention plans.

SKIN TESTS

Doctors use two types of skin tests to identify the cause of an allergic reaction: the scratch test and the intradermal test. In both types, a doctor introduces allergens to the skin and then evaluates the reaction.

Doctors use scratch tests and intradermal tests to check for allergies to pollens, molds, dust mites, animal dander, and some foods. Diluted liquids made from the actual allergen are used for the tests.

A doctor does a scratch test on the skin on your back, outer upper arm, or inner forearm. The doctor or nurse cleans the test area with alcohol and then marks it with a pen to indicate which allergen has been introduced at each location on your skin. The doctor will place a drop of each allergen on the corresponding mark. He or she will use a small disposable pricking device to scratch the skin, allowing the extract to enter the outer layer, or epidermis.

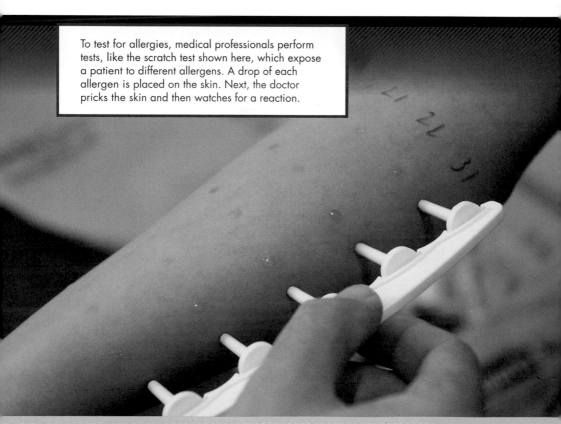

To test for allergies, medical professionals perform tests, like the scratch test shown here, which expose a patient to different allergens. A drop of each allergen is placed on the skin. Next, the doctor pricks the skin and then watches for a reaction.

In an intradermal test, the doctor or nurse injects the allergens under the skin. In both tests, after fifteen to twenty minutes, he or she checks the skin for a reaction. If a small red bump called a wheal develops, you are allergic to the allergen tested at that location on your skin. The area around the wheal also flares, or reddens. A wheal and a flare develop as a result of IgE antibodies causing mast cells to release histamine.

Occasionally, a more serious reaction can develop during skin testing. Severe swelling or itching, flushing of the skin, difficulty in breathing, a drop in blood pressure, or loss of consciousness may occur. Then the doctor will give an injection of epinephrine to reverse the reaction. For people with asthma, the skin test sometimes triggers an asthma attack, with wheezing, coughing, and tightness of the chest. This indicates that asthma is present and identifies the substance that triggers the asthma symptoms. Because skin tests sometimes lead to severe reactions, the doctor will ask you to wait in the office for at least thirty minutes after the test.

Positive test results must be considered in combination with the patient history and physical examination. You could be allergic to a substance even though it doesn't show up on your skin test. This is because skin tests do not always cause symptoms to develop.

For accurate results, you must tell your doctor about any medications you have taken and when you last took them. Taking antihistamines before undergoing a skin test can

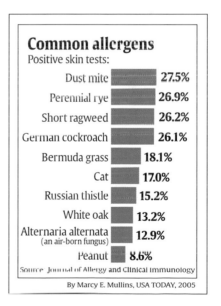

Common allergens
Positive skin tests:

Dust mite	27.5%
Perennial rye	26.9%
Short ragweed	26.2%
German cockroach	26.1%
Bermuda grass	18.1%
Cat	17.0%
Russian thistle	15.2%
White oak	13.2%
Alternaria alternata (an air-born fungus)	12.9%
Peanut	8.6%

Source: Journal of Allergy and Clinical Immunology

By Marcy E. Mullins, USA TODAY, 2005

lead to incorrect results. And some antihistamines can stay in your system for as long as a few weeks.

RADIOALLERGOSORBENT TEST

Doctors use this blood test, often called a RAST test, when skin testing might be dangerous, such as for someone who has had a severe allergic reaction to food. The RAST test is also useful for people who suffer from severe eczema (a skin condition) and have a rash over large areas of their skin.

In this test, a doctor or a nurse will take a blood specimen from the arm and send it to a laboratory. There, a technician checks for the presence of IgE antibodies. Although blood testing is safer than skin testing, it is less sensitive. It also is more limited because it tests for fewer allergenic substances than a skin test. So some allergies may be missed.

DIAGNOSING A FOOD ALLERGY

It can be tempting to diagnose a food allergy yourself. But only a medical doctor can accurately diagnose and treat food allergies. Self-diagnosis can lead to unnecessary dietary restrictions and inadequate nutrition. Physicians use several important tools to diagnose food allergies.

FOOD DIARY

For a week to a month, a doctor may have you write down everything you eat, how much of it you eat, when you eat it, and what reaction, if any, occurs. It is often helpful to write down even the brand names of the products you eat, since ingredients can differ from brand to brand. The doctor will then try to determine if a food causes a reaction each time it is eaten.

ELIMINATION DIET

If your doctor recommends an elimination diet, you remove the food suspected of causing the reaction from your diet for two to three weeks. Then the suspect food is once again added to the diet so that your body can become cleared of any food allergens that are still lingering. Your body can also recover completely from any symptoms that have appeared during past reactions. Then, with an allergen-free, symptom-free body, you once again eat the suspect food. A reaction at this time confirms the diagnosis. For example, if the doctor suspects that you are allergic to oats, then you would not be allowed to eat oatmeal, oat cereal, or cookies and cake made with oats. If a reaction occurs when the oats are added back into your diet two or three weeks later, the doctor can confirm the diagnosis that you are allergic to oats.

A doctor trying to diagnose a food allergy may ask patients to only eat foods such as bananas, lamb, rice, and applesauce. By introducing foods one by one back into a patients's diet, the doctor can determine which foods may be causing an allergic reaction.

If the problem food cannot be narrowed down to one particular food or a family of foods, the doctor may put you on a different type of elimination diet—one that is more restrictive. Perhaps you will eat only lamb, rice, bananas, and applesauce because these foods are not likely to cause an allergic reaction. When you are symptom-free, foods are added back into your diet one by one.

IS IT A FOOD ALLERGY?

Allergy experts say that people who have reactions to certain foods should sort out the causes of those reactions with their health-care provider. Different food-related problems may require different management techniques and treatments.

Food allergy: This is an immune system reaction that occurs soon after eating a certain food. Even a tiny amount of the allergy-causing food can trigger symptoms such as digestive problems, hives, or swollen airways. In some people, a food allergy can cause severe symptoms or even life-threatening anaphylaxis.

Food intolerance: This is much more common than a food allergy. Because a food intolerance can cause some of the same symptoms as a food allergy, people often confuse the two. Food intolerance generally doesn't involve the immune system. It can be caused by the absence of an enzyme needed to fully digest a food. A common example is lactose intolerance. Irritable bowel syndrome and sensitivity to certain additives also are examples of food intolerance.

Celiac disease: When a person with this immune system disease eats any food containing gluten, a type of protein found in wheat, inflammation in the small intestines occurs.

—USA Today, *January 7, 2010*
Sources: Mayo Clinic; Robert Wood, Johns Hopkins

An elimination diet must always be done under a doctor's supervision. If a suspected food has ever caused anaphylaxis, it should never be restored to your diet. You should strictly avoid it because even a small taste could cause a life-threatening reaction. If the reaction was mild, your doctor may suggest avoiding the suspected food for at least six months and then trying it in a very small amount. If you have no reaction, you may be able to eat this food occasionally and in moderation.

FOOD CHALLENGE

Your doctor may recommend a food challenge to confirm a specific food allergy. During this test, you eat the suspect food in small, increasing amounts. If a reaction occurs, it shows that a food allergy exists. When the doctor is not completely certain that a food allergen has caused your symptoms, a food challenge can show proof one way or the other. This test should be done only in the doctor's office or in the hospital in case a dangerous reaction develops. Strict medical supervision is always necessary during a food challenge.

TREATMENT

The best way to treat allergies is to prevent allergic reactions. Avoid the allergen or allergens that cause the reaction. However, allergens cannot always be avoided completely or enough to prevent a reaction. To help you manage your allergies, your doctor will set up a treatment program for you based on what causes your reaction and the severity of the reaction. Some symptoms respond well to medications. Yet not everyone can tolerate the side effects. Rely on your doctor's recommendations. The medication can be adjusted or changed during treatment, if necessary. In some cases, the doctor will choose to use immunotherapy, or allergy shots, as part of the treatment.

www.usatoday.com

USA TODAY

Life

SECTION D

March 22, 2010

From the Pages of USA TODAY

Allergy shots get best results; New methods might sway reluctant patients

The signs of spring are here. Trees are budding, grass is greening—and millions of allergy sufferers are taking pills, inhaling nasal sprays and avoiding the outdoors to control reactions that range from mild sniffles to dangerous asthma attacks.

Few, however, are using what may be the most effective treatment for uncontrolled symptoms: immunotherapy, or what most people know as allergy shots. The practice of injecting people with increasing amounts of the substances they are allergic to, so they can build gradual tolerance, is nearly 100 years old.

But U.S. surveys suggest shots are used by just 5% of nasal allergy patients.

"Inconvenience is the most likely reason," says Linda Cox, an allergist in Fort Lauderdale [Florida]. A typical treatment plan calls for a patient to come to a medical office once a week for several months, get a shot and wait 30 minutes (in case a rare, dangerous reaction occurs) and then continue less frequent shots for months or years more.

There's also a needle "fear factor," says Stanley Fineman, an Atlanta [Georgia] allergist and vice president of the American College of Allergy, Asthma & Immunology. And costs for the shots and office visits, which vary based on insurance coverage and other factors, may play a role.

But a recent study published in the *Annals of Allergy, Asthma and Immunology* showed children who get allergy shots had lower health care costs over 18 months than otherwise similar children. The cost of their shots, about $600, was more than made up by drug savings and fewer doctors' visits and hospitalizations, says Cox, who led the study. Immunotherapy also might help prevent asthma, a costly lifelong condition.

So allergists are working to make the shots more appealing. Most efforts fall into two categories: non-shot alternatives and faster shot schedules.

Liquid or pill alternatives

Immunotherapy without shots is standard in Europe. There, most doctors prescribe "sublingual immunotherapy." Patients get liquids or pills containing extracts of grass pollen, dust mites, ragweed or other allergens and put a bit under their tongues at home each day.

But none of these products has been approved by the U.S. Food and Drug Administration. Some U.S. physicians prescribe sublingual use of liquid extracts approved for injections—but that is an unproven practice. And some studies on sublingual products under development have failed to show they work better than placebos.

That is changing, though. In one new study, a daily sublingual grass pollen pill reduced symptoms and medication use 26% in children and teens, says Michael Blaiss, clinical professor of pediatrics and medicine at the University of Tennessee Health Science Center in Memphis. Blaiss,

a consultant to the drug's maker, Merck, presented the data at a recent meeting of the American Academy of Allergy, Asthma & Immunology. A study in adults found similar results, he says. The pills have not been compared with shots and might cost more. They are not available now.

What is increasingly available: faster shot schedules. In so-called rush immunotherapy, allergists give patients numerous shots over one to three days to quickly build tolerance so patients can soon start coming just once or twice a month. In the somewhat slower "cluster" technique, patients might come once or twice a week for a month and get two or three shots at each visit to get a faster start. These patients all get antihistamines, steroids or other drugs to prevent dangerous reactions.

Cox says the cluster technique is more widely used and thought safer. But Fineman says he safely gives rush patients nine to 20 injections in a day.

—Kim Painter

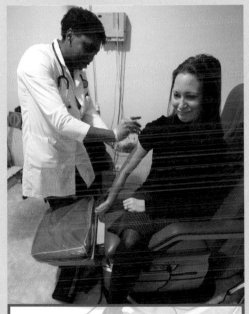

This patient is undergoing immunotherapy. She receives regularly scheduled allergy shots to desensitize her body to allergens.

MEDICATIONS

While there is no cure for allergies, some medications can help manage symptoms. Some medications are available without a prescription, but discuss your options with a doctor if symptoms are severe.

Epinephrine

Epinephrine saves lives during an allergic reaction. It stops the release of the chemical mediators responsible for causing symptoms. Doctors use it to reverse severe reactions involving the entire body, such as anaphylaxis. Epinephrine comes in a single-dose prefilled automatic injection device. During a severe allergic reaction, the drug is injected into the thigh.

Cromolyn Sodium

Cromolyn sodium is a preventive medication. It can prevent or minimize symptoms with daily use. Doctors often prescribe cromolyn sodium to treat allergic rhinitis, which causes inflammation of the nose, and asthma. This medication comes in a nasal spray and works by blocking the release of histamine and other chemical mediators. Cromolyn sodium is not effective once a reaction is under way.

Antihistamines

Antihistamines are the staple medications for relieving allergy symptoms. They work by competing with histamine for attaching at certain places in the body. They occupy the places in the nose, eyes, skin, and other sites that histamine would otherwise occupy. It's like the game of musical chairs. Once all the chairs are taken, someone is left out. So if an antihistamine medication occupies the sites that histamine would occupy during a reaction, no room is left for the histamine. Then the symptoms of sneezing, runny nose, itchy eyes, and rashes never develop.

Antihistamines are one type of medication patients suffering from allergies can take to relieve some of their symptoms.

Antihistamines are taken by mouth in pill or liquid form. Antihistamines are most effective when taken before an allergic reaction begins. They do also help if taken after symptoms occur. Some work in about thirty minutes. Others may take an hour or even a few days to work. It is best to take them regularly.

Decongestants

Decongestants work by narrowing blood vessels. This helps to shrink swollen mucous membranes and relieve nasal congestion. Decongestants are taken by mouth in pill or liquid form. Some are available in nasal sprays. Decongestants take effect in a few minutes and work well to relieve symptoms when an allergic reaction is already under way.

Corticosteroids

Corticosteroids are anti-inflammatory drugs that are highly effective in treating allergy symptoms. These are not the muscle-

Nasal sprays containing corticosteroids treat people with allergic rhinitis.

building types of steroids that some athletes use. Corticosteroid medications and muscle-building drugs are both steroids. But they are two separate types and are not related to each other.

Nasal corticosteroid spray medications are inhaled into the nostrils to decrease inflammation. They may take up to two weeks to begin working, so start using them before the onset of the allergy season. They are more effective when used regularly.

To treat allergic skin reactions, such as eczema, doctors prescribe topical corticosteroid creams and ointments. They soothe the skin by reducing inflammation and itching. Corticosteroid creams and ointments must be used cautiously and only as directed by a doctor. Side effects caused by overuse include thinning or aging of the skin and patchy lightening of normal skin color.

Oral corticosteroids (taken by mouth) are used to treat the symptoms of systemic allergic reactions, or those that involve the entire body. They are relatively safe for a short period in low doses. Their side effects can be serious, including elevated blood pressure, weight gain, and stunted growth (in children), when used over a long time and in high doses. If you need an oral corticosteroid to relieve your symptoms, your doctor will put you on the lowest dose possible and for the shortest time. Follow the instructions when taking this medication.

IMMUNOTHERAPY

Immunotherapy, also known as desensitization, or allergy shots, is an effective treatment for many allergies. Your doctor will turn to immunotherapy when medications have not relieved symptoms or when the side effects of medication are too severe. The therapy also helps when symptoms seriously interfere with activities or when the allergen can't be avoided.

Allergy shots help the immune system to tolerate allergens. So the body becomes less sensitive, or desensitized, to the offending substance.

Just as the body produces IgE antibodies, it also can produce IgE-blocking antibodies, or IgG antibodies. Immunotherapy forces the body to create IgG antibodies. The doctor injects a small amount of allergen. The body then produces IgG antibodies that prevent the allergen from attaching to the IgE antibodies. You will recall that the IgE antibodies cover the surfaces of mast cells and basophils. If the allergen does not attach to the IgE antibodies (like a key going into a car ignition), the mast cells and basophils cannot be turned on, or activated. If these cells are not activated, they will not release histamine and other chemical mediators that cause the symptoms of an allergic reaction.

During immunotherapy, a doctor or nurse injects you with an allergen extract. This liquid solution contains a tiny amount of the allergen. Allergen extracts are available for a variety of allergens. These include pollens, molds, dust mites, animal dander, and insect venom. They are not available for food or drugs. Injecting these allergens can be very dangerous. As with skin tests, you should wait thirty minutes before leaving the doctor's office in case you develop a severe reaction.

The doctor will begin with very small amounts of the allergen and then gradually increase the amounts until the doctor determines the

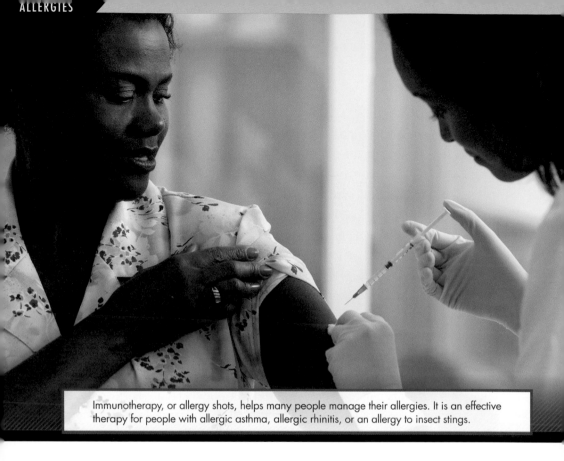

Immunotherapy, or allergy shots, helps many people manage their allergies. It is an effective therapy for people with allergic asthma, allergic rhinitis, or an allergy to insect stings.

maintenance dose. The maintenance dose is the amount at which continued injections throughout the year will prevent the outbreak of symptoms. You may get shots once or twice a week in the beginning and then every two to four weeks thereafter. Injections for life-endangering conditions, such as allergies to insect venom, sometimes continue throughout a patient's life. If you have more than one allergy, your doctor may choose to combine the allergens in one shot. Some doctors prefer to give separate shots for each allergen.

For immunotherapy to be effective, the proper amount of allergen must be injected into the body. Too little allergen and the body will not produce enough IgG antibodies. Too much allergen will overwhelm the body and trigger an allergic reaction that will involve the entire body. This type of reaction could be dangerous or even fatal. Your doctor will start with a small dose and then gradually increase the dose in subsequent injections.

Once your doctor determines the maintenance dose, your condition will improve. Continuing to receive your shots as often as your doctor recommends will make a difference in how effective the therapy is for you.

Allergy shots are not painful. The allergen is injected under the skin, not into the muscle. However, some redness and itching may appear at the injection site. After all, you are receiving a shot containing something to which you are allergic. Allergy shots do not cure allergies, and some symptoms may remain. But immunotherapy can make living with allergies a lot easier.

CHAPTER THREE

ALLERGIC RHINITIS

JAY'S STORY

Every spring, I suffered with allergies. My sinuses got blocked, my nose ran, and my eyes itched and watered. But nothing was as bad as the headaches. The misery usually went on for several weeks, and then, when summer began, I finally started to feel better. One of the worst parts about having allergies in the spring is that our school always gives placement tests and standardized tests at that time. I always ended up taking antihistamines and decongestants to relieve the congestion and headache, but then those medications made me really drowsy. So I couldn't win. I either had to take the tests feeling miserable, or I had to take them feeling sleepy.

The turning point came when I was in my room doing my homework one afternoon. I had such a bad headache that I couldn't concentrate. It was so bad I was almost in tears. My mom was worried and made an appointment with an allergist right away.

We found out that I'm allergic to oak and elm tree pollens. We have a lot of trees in our neighborhood, and there are woods behind my school. The doctor gave me some prescription medication, which not only worked a lot better than the over-the-counter medicine I was taking, but it didn't make me drowsy. The only thing that I still have trouble with is wearing my contact lenses during the allergy season. The contacts irritate my eyes, and I've ended up with eye infections. Now I just wear my glasses during pollen season, which has been working out well.

Is your nose stuffy and runny? Are your eyes itchy and watery? Do you feel pressure or pain in your ears? Does the roof of your

Sneezing, itchy eyes, scratchy throat, and a runny nose are symptoms of allergic rhinitis. This condition can be triggered by pollen in the air at different times of the year.

mouth itch? Does your head ache? Does your throat feel scratchy and itchy? Do you cough or clear your throat a lot? Do you sneeze five or ten times in a row? Do you feel irritable and tired?

These are the symptoms of allergic rhinitis, the most common allergy. The word *rhinitis* means "inflammation of the nose." When allergies cause this inflammation, allergic rhinitis occurs. The two forms of allergic rhinitis are seasonal and perennial. Both types seem to have a connection to asthma and eczema. People who have one of these conditions are likely to have another, although it is unusual to have all three.

SEASONAL ALLERGIC RHINITIS

The popular name for seasonal allergic rhinitis is hay fever. As Jay learned, hay fever is triggered seasonally, when trees, grasses, and weeds reproduce, or pollinate, and release millions of tiny pollen grains into the air we breathe. Mold spores also can cause hay fever symptoms.

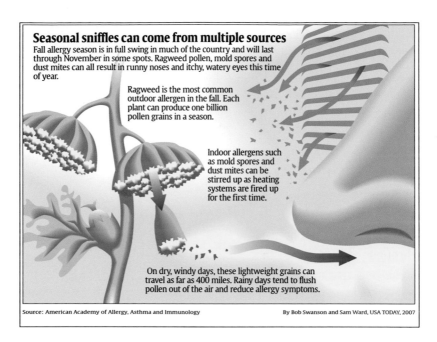

Seasonal sniffles can come from multiple sources

Fall allergy season is in full swing in much of the country and will last through November in some spots. Ragweed pollen, mold spores and dust mites can all result in runny noses and itchy, watery eyes this time of year.

Ragweed is the most common outdoor allergen in the fall. Each plant can produce one billion pollen grains in a season.

Indoor allergens such as mold spores and dust mites can be stirred up as heating systems are fired up for the first time.

On dry, windy days, these lightweight grains can travel as far as 400 miles. Rainy days tend to flush pollen out of the air and reduce allergy symptoms.

Source: American Academy of Allergy, Asthma and Immunology   By Bob Swanson and Sam Ward, USA TODAY, 2007

POLLENS

If you have ever seen a powdery yellow coating on a car or a pond, you have seen just how much pollen plants can release during their growing season. Some plants, such as ragweed, can release one million grains of pollen per plant each year. Pollination occurs at different times in different places. Generally trees release their pollen in late winter and spring, grasses in late spring and summer, and weeds in late summer and fall.

The minute grains of pollen travel through the air. Their numbers and direction depend on changes in temperature, humidity, and wind current. Pollen disperses best on a warm, breezy day, when the humidity is low. High humidity and heavy rains tend to slow down its distribution.

The size of the pollen grains makes a difference in how far pollens can travel and where they can settle. The pollen produced by colorful flowers is too large and heavy to float in the air. It is waxy and sticks to the bodies of bees, which carry it from plant to plant. The pollen produced by trees, grasses, and weeds is much smaller and lighter, however, and in much greater quantity. When weather conditions are right, it can easily travel through the air. In fact, some pollens can travel 400 miles (640 kilometers)! This ability to so easily become airborne causes all the trouble for allergy sufferers. The tiny specks of pollen that are floating through the air can enter the nose. This

In the spring, the catkins (flower clusters) of the hazel tree release clouds of pollen. This pollen causes problems for allergy sufferers.

sets the stage for the symptoms of allergic rhinitis to begin. And it is possible to be allergic to more than one pollen.

For an allergic reaction to take place, previous exposure to the pollen is necessary. Sensitization must occur before symptoms can appear. Once the body is exposed to a pollen allergen, the immune system treats it as an enemy and produces IgE antibodies in defense.

When the pollen enters the nose, the blood vessels expand and leak fluid, producing extra mucus. This causes inflammation and congestion. The nose becomes stuffy and runny. Mucus drips down the throat, a symptom known as postnasal drip. The nose tries to sneeze itself clear, while the throat tries to cough up the never-ending postnasal drip.

Meanwhile, the sinuses cannot drain because they are swollen and inflamed. This causes the head to ache. Congestion of the eustachian tube, the canal that connects the middle ear with the area in the back of the nose and throat, causes the ears to feel full and painful. Hearing is sometimes lessened. The eyes react by burning, itching, and swelling as a result of the histamine released by mast cells in the delicate conjunctivas, the mucous membranes that cover the front of the eyes and the inside of the eyelids. The eyes turn red and watery.

USA TODAY Snapshots®

Tips for allergy sufferers
Until the first frost, hay fever sufferers should:

▶ Keep windows closed at night and use air conditioning.
▶ Limit outdoor activity when pollen counts are highest and on windy days.
▶ Shower before going to sleep to avoid bringing pollen to bed.

Sources: American Academy of Allergy, Asthma and Immunology; AP

By Sam Ward, USA TODAY, 2002

Because the symptoms of allergic rhinitis are so similar to those of a cold, people who have these symptoms often think they have a cold. But there are some ways to distinguish one from the other:

- The nasal discharge of allergic rhinitis is watery and clear. It is thick and yellow or green in a cold.
- There is no fever with allergic rhinitis. A fever may accompany a cold.
- The eyes, ears, nose, and throat itch in allergic rhinitis. There is usually no itching with a cold.
- Sneezing in allergic rhinitis tends to happen in spells of five times or more. Sneezing is occasional in a cold.

People who have hay fever sometimes experience cross-reactivity. They react to foods that are closely related to specific pollen allergens. For example, people allergic to birch tree pollen sometimes find that their symptoms worsen when they eat apple skin. And people allergic to ragweed pollen sometimes find that their symptoms worsen when they eat cantaloupe or honeydew melon.

MOLDS

Mold is the microscopic form of fungi, which are nonflowering, parasitic plants. Because they do not have roots, stems, leaves, or chlorophyll (the green pigment in plants that absorbs light) molds must get their nourishment from other plant and animal material. Molds grow almost everywhere. They are especially common at the seashore, near lakes, and other damp environments. In rural farming areas, they thrive on the corn, wheat, and oats grown there. They flourish on decaying vegetation and wood, such as freshly cut grass, piles of leaves, compost heaps, and hay. The mold season typically is from April to November. The peak season depends on where you live.

Molds reproduce by making spores, which are released into the air. Like pollen, we inhale mold spores. So people who are allergic to molds suffer the same symptoms as people who are allergic to pollens.

AVOIDING AIRBORNE ALLERGENS

Here are some ways to reduce exposure to pollens and mold spores:
- Limit outdoor activities during the early morning hours of the pollen season. The amount of pollen in the air is greater at this time, especially on dry, windy days.
- Keep the windows of the house and car closed. Use an air conditioner and clean the filter frequently. High-efficiency particulate air (HEPA) filters work well to trap pollens and molds.

www.usatoday.com

USA TODAY

Life
SECTION D

August 23, 2010

From the Pages of USA TODAY

Allergies? Maybe not; Those symptoms could be from non-allergic rhinitis

If you have a drippy or congested nose today, you've got lots of company.

After all, it's late August, and in much of the country, it's hay fever season or, more accurately, ragweed and mold allergy season. But if the symptoms get bad enough to send you to an allergist, you might get a surprise: You might not have allergies at all.

You could, of course, have a cold—and some adults get so many they are convinced they've developed an allergy, doctors say. One hint to their true condition, says Albany, N.Y., allergist David Shulan: They often are teachers or parents.

"They're really just catching a lot of colds from kids," he says.

But there's another possibility, one many people have never heard of: It's called "non-allergic rhinitis."

People with non-allergic rhinitis have many of the same symptoms as people with nasal allergies—the runny noses, congestion and annoying postnasal drip. Some sneeze, too. But "when we do allergy testing on them, we don't find anything," Shulan says.

These patients often have no personal or family history of allergy and are older than the usual new allergy patient, averaging about age 35, says Jonathan Bernstein, an allergy researcher at the University of Cincinnati [Ohio]. They are more often women than men, he says.

Patients often say they have symptoms year-round or are bothered by irritants

- When outdoors, avoid areas with tall grass and weeds. Keep the grass in your yard cut short to prevent it from flowering and releasing pollen.
- After being outdoors for a long period, take a shower, wash your hair, and change your clothes.
- Wash clothes that are worn outdoors and then dry them in a dryer. Clothes that are hung out on a line will accumulate pollens and mold spores.

that are not known to cause the immune system responses associated with a true allergy, says Michael Blaiss, an allergist at the University of Tennessee Health Science Center in Memphis. The possible triggers include:

- Perfumes and other substances with strong odors.
- Cigarette smoke and car exhaust.
- Cold air, wind and high humidity.
- Foods—and not just the spicy ones (this variation is called gustatory rhinitis).

Just lying down triggers symptoms in some people, Blaiss says. Although these people don't have allergies, "this is a real condition," he says. "Some are suffering more than the patients I see with allergies."

Bernstein says: "It can have an impact on sleep and concentration, cause headaches and lead to sinus infections."

The underlying causes are not well understood. In some people, the problem seems related to changes in the nose that occur with aging, says Stanley Fineman, an Atlanta [Georgia] allergist and vice president of the American College of Allergy, Asthma & Immunology. Older noses tend to be drier, he says, so sometimes simple saline nose sprays can help.

Doctors also often recommend certain antihistamines, decongestants, steroid nasal sprays and drying agents. But the popular non-sedating antihistamines sold in drugstores often don't work, Blaiss says. Patients also won't benefit from allergy shots—unless they also have some allergies, which is possible, he adds.

It should be noted that adults can, at any age, develop new allergies or redevelop allergy symptoms that faded decades earlier, says Jacqueline Eghrari-Sabet, an allergist in Gaithersburg, Maryland. Sensitive people who move to new areas with high pollen counts often get new symptoms after two or three years of exposure. The best way to sort it all out, she says: Go to an allergist and get a skin test.

—Kim Painter

PERENNIAL ALLERGIC RHINITIS

The symptoms of year-round allergic rhinitis are the same as those of seasonal allergic rhinitis except that they do not come and go with the change of seasons. Instead, the symptoms continue all year and they tend to be worse indoors than outdoors. This is because allergens found inside the house cause year-round allergic rhinitis. These include indoor molds; house dust and decaying house dust mites; decaying cockroaches; and the dander, saliva, and urine of animals.

MOLDS

The mold spores that float through the air outdoors can end up inside the house and grow there. They especially love the damp, dark areas of a house. Some of their favorite places to live include basements, kitchens and bathrooms, laundry rooms, and garbage cans. Unlike outdoor molds, indoor molds are present all year. They constantly reproduce and release their spores into the air inside the house. For people who are allergic to molds, this is disastrous. Their symptoms will persist throughout the year.

You can use several strategies to cut down the amount of mold growing in your house. Use a household cleanser to kill the mold you can see, such as between bathroom tiles or around the kitchen sink. Get rid of old mildewed books and magazines. Remove old wallpaper and use a dehumidifier. Some people who are allergic to inhaled mold spores also react to eating foods that contain molds, such as cheese, dried fruits, olives, and cider. They react with gastrointestinal problems. For others, touching molds causes a skin reaction.

HOUSE DUST AND DUST MITES

House dust is more than just a powdery substance that coats furniture, books, floors, and other surfaces around the house. It is a blend of dried food particles, dried insect parts and droppings, upholstery and carpet lint, clothing lint, animal dander, and even tiny flakes of human skin. Flakes of skin are food for dust mites. These insects belong to the spider and tick family. Dust mites live and thrive in warm, humid environments where there are lots of human skin cells to feed on. A house is the perfect place. They invade carpeting, upholstered furniture, clothing, bedding, and even stuffed toys in their quest for nourishment. And they multiply quickly, producing a new generation every three weeks. Dust mites never live on people, so they do not bite and do not spread disease. They are harmful only to people who are allergic to them.

The droppings that dust mites leave behind decay and fill the air we breathe. When dust mites die, their bodies also decay and end up in the air. The decaying droppings and body parts are potent allergens. When an allergic person inhales them, they cause the symptoms of allergic rhinitis.

Some ways to control dust mites in your house include the following:

- Cover mattresses, box springs, and pillows with allergen-proof casings.
- Every week, wash sheets, blankets, and bedspreads in hot water (more than 130°F, or 54°C). This water is hot enough to scald you, so be careful.
- Remove carpeting from floors and use wood or tile instead. Washable area rugs must be washed frequently in hot water to kill the dust mites.
- Use window shades or washable curtains rather than draperies or venetian blinds.
- Get rid of under-the-bed storage, canopy beds, and pictures hanging on the wall. Vacuum the bedroom, including closets, once a week.
- Do not use down comforters, pillows, or jackets.
- Keep books in closed bookcases.
- Keep air conditioner and furnace filters clean.

COCKROACHES

The cockroach is another insect that causes problems for some people. The decaying bodies of dead cockroaches and their droppings get into the air we breathe, causing misery for those who are allergic to them.

Restaurants and grocery stores, especially in cities, are often infested with cockroaches. So are many homes. People in city environments tend to suffer most because the houses and buildings are close together and cockroaches can move freely among them. If cockroaches have moved into your home, you can get rid of them in a number of ways:

- Use roach traps, bait, or powder to kill the living cockroaches.
- Thoroughly clean the house after the insects are dead to clear the area before the bodies decay.
- Use caulking to close up any holes in walls and floors and around plumbing pipes. Cockroaches can enter the house through these holes. And cockroaches are attracted to moisture, so also repair any leaky faucets.
- Keep all food stored in closed containers. Wash and dry all dishes and utensils immediately after using them so as not to attract cockroaches.
- Do not store paper grocery bags, cardboard boxes, newspapers, or empty bottles in the house. Cockroaches like to live in these.

ANIMAL DANDER

Contrary to popular belief, the cause of pet allergies is not animal hair. Instead, animal dander, saliva, and urine are the culprits. Millions of tiny dander particles fall off pets' skin, hair, and feathers every day and become airborne. Because they are so small, dander particles can float around for many hours. Animal saliva and urine dry out on carpets and furniture and then flake off and become airborne, just as the dander does. Particles of dander, saliva, and urine are inhaled into the nose and lungs. There they will cause a reaction in those who are allergic.

Individuals with a family history or personal history of hay fever, asthma, or eczema seem to be especially prone to pet allergies. Many of these people are allergic to more than one kind of pet. For some people, just being around products made from animals, such as wool or down bedding or clothing, can be a problem.

People often think that one breed of dog or cat is better than another in not causing an allergic reaction. This is not true. Since animal hair is not the problem, a short-haired dog is no better than a long-haired one. Cats seem to cause more allergic reactions than dogs. Doctors believe this is because cats constantly lick and groom themselves, allowing more of their saliva to dry and become airborne.

People can be allergic to horses, rabbits, gerbils, hamsters, guinea pigs, and mice. The droppings of birds and other caged pets (rabbits, hamsters, guinea pigs, gerbils, and mice) can be a source of dust and mold. If you already have a pet and cannot give it up, you can lower the level of allergens in your house: keep the pet out of rooms where you spend the most time, such as the bedroom and the family room; brush your cat or dog regularly; and clean your cat's litter box, your bird's cage, or any other pet cages frequently

Although taking measures to reduce the animal and bird allergens in the house will help in managing your allergies, it will not solve the problem. The best pets for people who have allergies are reptiles, fish, and hermit crabs

Fish are good pets for people who are allergic to animal dander.

DIAGNOSING ALLERGIC RHINITIS

Because many nonallergic conditions have symptoms much like those of allergic rhinitis, it is best to start with a patient history. The doctor will want to know when your nose gets congested or runny, what the mucus looks like, when your sneezing begins, and when the itching begins. A physical examination will rule out other causes for your symptoms, such as a sinus infection.

If the doctor suspects an allergy to pollens or mold spores, the doctor will confirm the diagnosis with skin tests and blood tests. When the doctor suspects that something in your home causes your symptoms, you may be asked to keep a diary of exactly what your symptoms are and when, where, how often, and under what circumstances they occur. Then a skin test and blood test can confirm the diagnosis.

TREATMENT

Avoidance of the allergen is the most effective treatment. If the allergen is something in your house, concentrate on keeping your bedroom as free of the allergen as possible. Because you may sleep approximately eight hours a night, you will spend the most time in this room. Other buildings, including schools, are also filled with allergens. During the school year, you are surrounded by pollens, molds, dust, and dust mites. So even if you are able to avoid your allergen at home, you may not be able to do so at school.

Whether you are able to avoid your allergen or not, medications can help you manage your symptoms. Your doctor may recommend that you use cromolyn sodium or antihistamines before symptoms start. Decongestants can help relieve nasal congestion once a reaction has already begun. The doctor will decide which of these drugs you should use.

If these medications do not help, the doctor may turn to a corticosteroid medication. Some nasal sprays and eye drops contain corticosteroids. In some cases, the doctor may recommend allergy shots. For people who are not helped by medication or who cannot tolerate the medication, allergy shots are the only relief.

If you do not treat allergic rhinitis, other medical conditions may develop. Sinusitis (inflammation of a sinus), ear infections and hearing loss, nasal polyps (fluid-filled pockets on the lining of the nose), loss of taste and smell, and asthma are among the complications that can occur. See a doctor and receive appropriate treatment for allergic rhinitis before these other problems set in.

ALLERGIC RHINITIS AND AIR POLLUTION

Air pollution and strong odors can trigger allergic rhinitis. Outdoors, the air we breathe contains gases such as carbon monoxide, sulfur dioxide, nitrogen dioxide, ozone, and lead. These contaminants come from power plants, petroleum refineries, factories, and motor vehicle and airplane exhaust.

Smokestacks of chemical plants release pollution into the air. Air pollution is one cause of allergic rhinitis and other upper respiratory conditions.

December 6, 2006

From the Pages of USA TODAY

Activists use research to win pollution battles

The buses idle along 146th Street, the faint smell of diesel exhaust in the air. The weathered brick bus depot sits across the street from day care and recreation centers for seniors and children.

Millicent Redick raised a son and daughter here in Harlem [New York], across the street from the city's Mother Clara Hale Bus Depot. She recalls how they both suffered from eczema and asthma. "I was always led to believe that I had to keep the dust out of my apartment, so I cleaned all the time," says Redick, 61, a retired accountant. "But I was never informed that the air we were breathing played a role. . . . I thought it was all me."

Then she learned of connections between pollution and asthma attacks, and cleaning up the air became her new mission. "I've always felt strongly that no matter where I live, I have a right to everything every other community has," she says. "That's what I fought for."

Five of Manhattan's six bus depots are north of 96th Street. The struggle by residents and activists against that concentration is one of many environmental battles being waged around the nation in a campaign to improve the health and safety of poor and minority communities.

"People are not . . . taking the poison quietly," says Robert Bullard, director of Clark Atlanta University's Environmental Justice Resource Center and author of the book *Dumping in Dixie: Race, Class, and Environmental Quality*. "Over the last decade

Indoors, many chemicals fill the air: fumes from gas or oil furnaces, pilot lights on gas stoves, paints, nail polish, scented candles, air fresheners, scented lotions, perfumes, colognes, soaps and laundry detergents, and cleaning solutions. Smoke from fireplaces, wood-burning stoves, and cigarettes also ends up in the air we breathe, as do fumes from carpeting, insulation, glues, dyes, and solvents used in or so, not only do you have communities fighting, but they also have developed alliances and coalitions with scientists and lawyers and economists."

Neighborhood activists from California to Washington, D.C., are using a growing body of research on how pollutants [worsen] illness to block the building of facilities, relocate residents from contaminated communities and gain other concessions from large firms.

"One of the problems with all environmental struggles, but particularly when you have the overlay of environmental racism, is the community always has the burden of proof of harm," says Elizabeth Crowe, an organizer with the Kentucky Environmental Foundation in Berea, Kentucky. Now, "we have much more definitive information as to how bad this stuff is. . . . So the science is catching up to the experiences of folks on the ground, and it helps prove the point."

High asthma rates

Upper Manhattan's bus depots, many of them former trolley barns, have been around for nearly a century. The New York City Council's transportation committee held a hearing in October on the concentration of bus depots in Harlem, which has the city's highest rate of asthma hospitalizations for children 14 and younger, according to the city Department of Health and Mental Hygiene. The department says diesel particulates have been proved to worsen asthma.

"We think [the depots are] very, very responsible for the high asthma rates in the community," says Kizzy Charles-Guzman, policy coordinator of the group WE ACT for Environmental Justice. "It goes beyond air quality. . . . It's also quality of life impact. You have constant noise and vibrations from the buses, and we also have sanitation truck depots and sewage treatment facilities. . . . We're not necessarily saying let's shut down the depots and move them all over the city, but if all the clean buses the [bus agency] claims to have in the fleet were assigned to these particular depots, that would help."

—*Charisse Jones*

building materials. For people with allergic rhinitis, this chemical blend can magnify the problems they already face in managing their condition.

This is a bigger problem for people who live in cities. Preventive measures include exercising indoors and minimizing time spent outdoors. This is especially important in the summer months when air quality in cities is at its worst.

CHAPTER FOUR

SKIN ALLERGIES

LYNN'S STORY

The skin on my hands was always so red and sore and really rough. I dreaded having to shake anyone's hand because I felt embarrassed about how horrible my hands must have looked to other people, and I felt humiliated at school knowing that my hands were so disgusting.

My skin was unbearably itchy. The itch was so bad sometimes that I scratched until I bled. When it itched like that, it felt just like a really itchy mosquito bite. Once I started scratching it, I couldn't stop. I just wanted to scratch until the itch went away. My hands would be really sore for a few days, and then they would heal and I would think everything was okay. But then it would start all over again. Once, I was in the grocery store with my mom, and a little kid said, "Eew, what's wrong with your hands?" I was so hurt, I just burst into tears. That's when my mom decided to take me to the doctor.

The doctor asked me several questions and then looked at the rash. She said she thought my problem was eczema, and she said there was a chance it was related to food allergies. I couldn't think of any food that made my problem worse when I ate it, but I didn't know my problem could be related to food, so I wasn't really paying attention to that. The doctor put me on a very restricted diet for a couple of weeks, and I didn't have any flare-ups during that time. Then foods were added back into my diet, one at a time. I was shocked to find out that my hands got red and itchy when we added cheese. Now I try to stay away from it as much as possible. Every now and then, I cheat, and then I have to go through the itching and scratching. My doctor gave me a cream to use when I have flare-ups, and she recommended a mild soap to use. They've helped a lot to control the itching.

The skin protects the body. It comes in contact with foreign substances, some of which are harmful. Skin acts as a barrier against these substances. Some people's skin becomes inflamed or blistered a day or two after coming into contact with substances such as poison ivy or poison oak, cosmetics, metals (such as nickel used in some cell phones, jewelry, and zippers), or household chemicals. The skin eruptions are caused by an adverse (negative) reaction to these substances. Usually, the symptoms of a skin allergy are patches of flaky skin, itchy red bumps and rashes, or swelling. But in people who are allergic to latex rubber, coming in contact with the substance can cause anaphylaxis.

ATOPIC DERMATITIS, OR ECZEMA

Eczema, the skin condition that Lynn has, often begins in infancy or early childhood. Symptoms include extremely itchy patches of skin that are dry, red, and flaky. These itchy patches can appear almost anywhere on the body. They are particularly common on skin folds, such as inside the elbows or behind the knees. The face, back of the hands and feet, and the neck are other common sites. Symptoms tend to come and go. They may fade to just a tiny patch but then spread out again and cover large areas of the body. The condition is often worse in winter, when the air is dry.

Skin affected by eczema can easily become infected because it is so dry, scaly, and itchy. It just begs to be scratched. Stress and sweating tend to intensify the itch. Lots of scratching eventually can cause the skin to break open, allowing bacteria to enter. And then the infection makes the skin itch all the more. The cycle can become vicious. Oozing, crusting, and swelling indicate that infection has set in. Once the infection begins, it can spread from small areas to large areas and become a generalized skin infection.

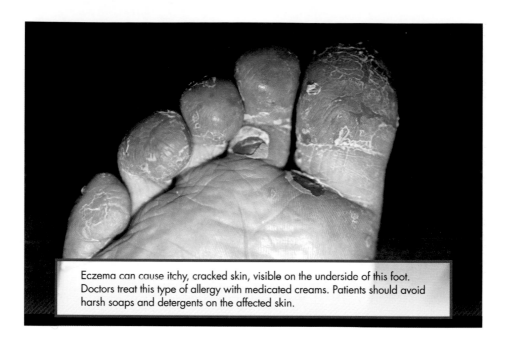

Eczema can cause itchy, cracked skin, visible on the underside of this foot. Doctors treat this type of allergy with medicated creams. Patients should avoid harsh soaps and detergents on the affected skin.

The bacteria must be treated with antibiotics prescribed by your doctor. Controlling the itching, keeping your fingernails trimmed, and keeping your body clean are ways to help prevent serious skin infections. When eczema is present for a long time, lichenification can result, in which the skin becomes thick, hard, and brownish.

DIAGNOSIS

The best way to diagnose eczema is by using the patient history, the physical examination, and test results. The doctor will ask you questions to determine whether the condition is eczema or another skin problem. Here are some of the questions your doctor may ask:

- Is your rash itchy?
- Does your rash seem to come and go but with repeated flare-ups?

- Do you have more itching and rash during the winter months?
- Does your skin itch more when you feel stressed and when you perspire?
- Do you or any of your family members have allergic rhinitis or asthma?

Next, you will undergo a physical examination. The doctor will look for the following signs of eczema:
- Patches of rashy skin have darkened, thickened, and become scaly.
- A rash is on parts of the body commonly affected by eczema, such as the face, hands, neck, folds of the arms, and backs of the knees.
- Dermographism has occurred (the skin can be written on by scratching it with a dull instrument).

If information from the patient history and physical examination lead the doctor to suspect eczema, testing can confirm the diagnosis. These include skin tests, blood tests, and tests for food allergy.

SKIN TESTS

If your eczema appears to be related to inhaled allergens, skin tests sometimes can be helpful. Positive results on skin tests for pollens, molds, or animal dander can indicate that the skin condition is eczema. But the skin of people with eczema tends to show a reaction to a substance even when no true allergy to that substance exists. This means that the skin test may show sensitivity to inhaled allergens to which you are not really allergic. These are called false-positive results. Because skin test results are sometimes false positives, the doctor must consider test results in combination with other information and not rely on the test results alone.

BLOOD TESTS

If your skin is very rashy, the doctor will have to do a blood test instead of a skin test. The RAST blood test will show an elevation of IgE antibodies in your blood if an allergy is present. This confirms that the skin condition is eczema.

FOOD ALLERGY TESTS

If food allergy is believed to play a part in your eczema, the doctor can use an elimination diet, as Lynn's doctor did. This diet allows you to eat only a few foods for about two weeks. If you see improvement during this time, the link to food allergy is conclusive. Then foods are restored to your diet one at a time or one group at a time (breads and pasta, for example) to see if a reaction occurs. Using the elimination diet is a more drawn-out way to determine the culprit food. But this type of test is more reliable than skin testing.

TREATMENT

Eczema cannot be cured. Some people do outgrow it, but until then, it can be a chronic problem. It returns again and again. There are ways to control the symptoms, however. The most successful treatment is medication and avoiding contact with substances that trigger symptoms, such as food or inhaled allergens.

The doctor can prescribe a corticosteroid cream to be applied to the affected areas and an oral antihistamine to relieve the itching. If the symptoms are severe, oral corticosteroids may be prescribed. Allergy shots are not recommended for people with eczema because they often make the condition worse.

Break the cycle of itching and scratching to control the symptoms of eczema. Here are some things that will help:

- Avoid harsh soaps, detergents, lotions, and perfume.

- Avoid overdrying or chapping your skin. Long showers or baths and hot water can dry the skin. Do not use a washcloth or bath sponge for bathing. These can cause itching from rubbing the skin.
- After bathing, pat your skin dry with a towel. Immediately apply a hypoallergenic moisturizer to lock in the moisture from the shower or bath water.
- Before and after swimming in a pool, coat your body with a hypoallergenic moisturizer to prevent the chlorine in the water from drying your skin.
- Avoid wool fabrics, which are scratchy. Avoid synthetic fabrics, which may not absorb perspiration.
- In cold weather, keep the air from becoming dry inside the house during heating season. A humidifier or shallow pans of water placed near radiators can help. Change the water daily to prevent mold growth.
- Try to avoid excessive sweating, which can irritate the skin.
- If your skin is oozing, apply cold-water compresses to relieve itching and inflammation.
- Avoid sunburn and high humidity. They can worsen the rash, although moderate exposure to the sun can often help.

URTICARIA (HIVES) AND ANGIOEDEMA (SWELLING)

You probably know urticaria by its more common name, hives. Hives are itchy red bumps that can be small, like mosquito bites, or very large, sometimes measuring several inches in diameter. They can appear anywhere on the surface of the skin. They may be clustered in one area, especially where clothing is tight (the waistline, for example). In other cases, they may be widespread over the entire body.

www.usatoday.com

USA TODAY

Life
SECTION D

November 11, 2010

From the Pages of USA TODAY

"Cellphone rash" likely due to nickel allergy

If you're an incessant cellphone user and a mysterious rash appears along your jaw, cheek or ear, chances are you're allergic to nickel, a metal commonly used in cellphones.

While allergists have long been familiar with nickel allergy, "cellphone rash" is just starting to show up on their radar screen, said Dr. Luz Fonacier, head of allergy and immunology at Winthrop University Hospital in Mineola, N.Y.

"Increased use of cellphones with unlimited usage plans has led to prolonged exposure to the nickel in phones," said Fonacier, who discussed the condition in a larger presentation on skin allergies this weekend at the American College of Allergy, Asthma and Immunology annual meeting in Phoenix [Arizona].

Symptoms of cellphone allergy include a red, bumpy, itchy rash in areas where the nickel-containing parts of a cellphone touch the face. It can even affect fingertips of those who text continuously on buttons containing nickel. In severe cases, blisters and itchy sores can develop.

Fonacier said she sees many patients who are allergic to nickel and don't know it. "They come in with no idea of what is causing their allergic reaction," said Fonacier, also a professor of clinical medicine at the State

People who are allergic to nickel may develop so-called cell phone rash where the phone touches the skin. The nickel in the devices can irritate the skin.

University of New York at Stony Brook. Sometimes, she traces her patients' symptoms to their cellphones.

In 2000, a researcher in Italy documented the first case of cellphone rash, prompting other research on the condition. In a 2008 study published in the *Canadian Medical Association Journal*, U.S. researchers tested for nickel in 22 handsets from eight manufacturers; 10 contained the metal. The parts with the most nickel were the menu buttons, decorative logos on the headsets and the metal frames around the liquid crystal display (LCD) screens.

Cellphone rash is still not well known, said allergist Dr. Stanley M. Fineman, a clinical associate professor at the Emory University School of Medicine in Atlanta. While he's treated more cases of nickel allergy caused by piercings than by cellphones, "it's good for allergists and dermatologists to have cellphone contact dermatitis on their radar screens," he said.

Nickel allergy affects an estimated 17% of women and 3% of men. Women typically develop cellphone rash more often because they are more likely to have been sensitized to nickel after ear piercing, or had an allergic reaction to nickel-containing jewelry. If you get rashes from costume jewelry or the metal button on your jeans, you're probably nickel-sensitive, said Fonacier.

To treat cellphone rash, you can apply a mild over-the-counter corticosteroid, she said. (Ask your doctor about how long you can safely use it.) Then, keep the nickel-bearing parts of your phone off your face.

"Buy a phone cover, opt for a hands-free device, use the speaker phone or switch to a phone that doesn't contain nickel on surfaces that touch your skin," she said. Consult an allergist if the rash lingers.

If you know you're nickel-allergic, go online and order a nickel spot-test kit before you buy a new phone, Fonacier suggested. "Put a drop of the liquid (dimethylglyoxime) on a cotton swab and dab the swab on those parts of the phone where nickel is typically found," she said. "If the applicator turns pink, the phone contains a good amount of nickel."

Some researchers believe the United States should regulate nickel more stringently, as some European countries do, said Fonacier. Since 1994, the EU Nickel Directive has limited nickel release from consumer products that come into direct, prolonged contact with skin. Since then, the prevalence of nickel sensitivity has gone down in Germany and Denmark, according to studies published by researchers in those countries.

—Julia Vantine

www.usatoday.com

USA TODAY

Life

SECTION D

April 8, 2008

From the Pages of USA TODAY

Under the skin of color; Patients' ethnicity can change face of dermatology

White dermatologists didn't understand her skin, says Nakia Smith, 25, a longtime eczema sufferer. It was not until she visited Philadelphia [Pennsylvania] dermatologist Susan Taylor, who, like Smith, is a woman of color, that the dry, scaly patches on her face and arms cleared up.

"I had tried 50 million creams and was even told I'd just have to live with the eczema, but Dr. Taylor suggested things no one else had before. She understands my skin," says the postal worker and student in Lawnside, N.J.

Taylor is among a rising tide of dermatologists and spa owners who focus on the skin, hair and nail needs of women and men of color. Taylor, a spokeswoman for the American Academy of Dermatology, says all dermatologists should be well-versed in the differences between fair and dark skin.

"The demographics of our country are really changing, and many people of color are looking for a dermatologist familiar with their needs, even in the heartland, not just the metropolitan areas," Taylor says.

Easier to irritate brown skin

There's a definite need for such a specialty, says Rebat Halder, professor and chairman of the department of dermatology at Howard University in Washington, D.C. By

Hives, also called wheals, normally last no more than twenty-four hours. During that time, they tend to disappear and then reappear. They may appear in one place, disappear after a short time, and then reappear in another place. Hives may or may not be related to allergies, but when they are, foods, drugs, insect stings, and animal dander are the likely causes.

Angioedema is a condition that is similar to hives, but the swelling occurs beneath the skin. Angioedema often accompanies

2050, Halder says, half the population in the USA will be either African-American, Hispanic, Asian or Native American. According to the U.S. Census Bureau, about one-third of the population now has skin of color.

Brown skin contains more melanin, or dark pigment, Taylor says. She says melanin levels vary dramatically among the ethnic groups.

Cells called melanocytes make the melanin. Melanocytes, the cells in the upper layer of the skin, are more reactive in darker skin and can release more melanin when they're irritated, says Hema Sundaram, a dermatologist in the Washington area.

"Any type of irritation to dark skin—an ingrown hair, acne or a poor laser treatment—can cause dark discoloration, called hyperpigmentation, that will last for months, even years," says Sundaram, who notes that scars on white skin tend to be pink and resolve more quickly.

In whites, for example, washing the hair often helps clear up dandruff, while black women who shampoo daily may exacerbate a dry scalp and hair and cause increased breakage.

Who needs an expert?

Sundaram, a laser expert who has conducted research and lectured on the topic, says: "With brown skin, you need to use appropriate lasers and modified settings to avoid burns and discoloration.

"You may also need to be less aggressive with facial peels because taking off too many layers at once can lead to scarring."

Even women with the same brown skin tone but different cultural backgrounds may react differently to the same procedures, says Flor Mayoral, a dermatologist in Miami. Mayoral recommends that patients ask to have a test spot done before having a full skin procedure.

Mayoral, who is of Hispanic heritage, also advises patients to make sure their dermatologist "knows who you are, your ethnic background."

—*Mary Brophy Marcus*

hives, but it is possible to have one condition without the other. Angioedema involves swelling, especially of the eyes and lips. An entire arm, leg, or face may also swell. Angioedema may even occur in a person's throat or in his or her stomach. Swelling in the throat can cause airway obstruction. Swelling in the stomach can cause nausea, vomiting, abdominal pain, and diarrhea. Probable causes of angioedema include allergies to animal dander, foods, and insect bites.

DIAGNOSIS

Viral infections, intestinal parasites, and other diseases sometimes cause hives and angioedema. For this reason, the doctor must determine whether the hives are allergic or nonallergic. A patient history and physical examination are the most useful tools in making a diagnosis. The presence of the following factors can indicate an allergic reaction:

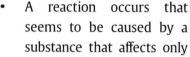

Allergic reactions sometimes include hives, which are red raised welts on the surface of the skin.

- A reaction occurs that seems to be caused by a substance that affects only a small percentage of people (for example, hives caused by eating a certain food).
- The patient had previous exposure to the substance without a reaction.
- The symptoms worsen with each reaction.

The doctor may ask you to keep a food diary or undergo a skin test to pinpoint the allergen.

TREATMENT

The best treatment for hives and angioedema is avoidance of the offending substance. In some cases, such as when airborne allergens or insect sting allergens cause the hives, allergy shots can help. Once an outbreak of hives is under way, topical corticosteroid creams can help the rash. Oral antihistamines can relieve the itch. The doctor may prescribe oral corticosteroids for severe cases.

Hives can be the first sign of a life-threatening anaphylactic reaction. If shortness of breath, wheezing, difficulty in swallowing, nausea, weakness, or confusion occurs after the outbreak of hives, you must seek emergency medical treatment immediately.

LATEX RUBBER ALLERGY

Latex is the milky sap from rubber trees, which grow in the tropics. It is used to make surgical gloves, dishwashing gloves, adhesive bandages, condoms, rubber bands, balloons, toys, and even pencil erasers. Fabrics with spandex also contain latex, as do the hand grips on many bicycles and racquets. Repeatedly coming into contact with latex provides the sensitization necessary to set the stage for an allergic reaction. Most allergic reactions are rashes, but some people experience anaphylaxis and even death.

DIAGNOSIS

In diagnosing a latex allergy, the doctor may do a "use" test. A latex rubber glove or the fingers of the glove are worn on the hands for fifteen to thirty minutes. The area then is checked for the development of a rash. This test should be done under a doctor's supervision because the test can cause anaphylaxis.

TREATMENT

Avoidance is best. If the rash is mild and latex is avoided, the rash will clear up within a few days. When the rash is severe, the doctor will prescribe a topical corticosteroid cream or an oral corticosteroid.

CHAPTER FIVE

FOOD ALLERGIES

PAUL'S STORY

A few years ago, I went with a friend to a party at the pool he belongs to. They had a table set up with snack food, like chocolate chip cookies, tortilla chips and salsa, pretzels, and potato chips. My friends and I were talking to a bunch of people and eating snacks. While we were standing there, I started to feel a little queasy and my nose started to itch and get stopped up. I thought I had been in the pool too long and the chlorine had irritated my sinuses. Then somebody said, "You have red spots all over you!" I looked down and saw hives on my chest and arms. They started to really itch, so I called my dad to pick me up. By the time he got there, I had really bad stomach cramps. He drove me straight to the emergency room because he thought I had food poisoning. By the time we got there, I was having trouble breathing and I felt like I was going to pass out. The doctor gave me a shot, and then everything was okay. He told my dad that the reaction I had was from an allergy, not from food poisoning, and he suggested that I see an allergist.

The allergist asked me a lot of questions about the foods I had eaten at the party, and then she said she suspected that there had been nuts in the chocolate chip cookies. She did a blood test and determined that I'm allergic to walnuts. I was really surprised because I had eaten walnuts many times and never had a problem. Ever since then, I've had to strictly avoid them. I have to read the labels on everything I eat. I also have to carry an EpiPen when I eat somewhere other than at home. I even have to keep one in the nurse's office at school in case something happens during lunch. I don't buy anything from the cafeteria. So far, I've been really careful and I've been okay.

Food allergies do not cause all bad reactions to food. Bacteria grows on food before it is cooked, and sometimes after. When bacteria enters our bodies, it can make us sick and can even cause death in some cases. Many food allergy symptoms are similar to the symptoms of a bacterial infection. Nausea, severe vomiting, stomach cramping, and diarrhea are symptoms commonly associated with both food allergy and bacterial infection. But food allergy can cause other symptoms as well, including hives, eczema, headache, a stuffy and itchy nose, and sneezing. Food allergy also can cause anaphylaxis, as it did with Paul.

Unless the immune system is involved, the reaction is not allergic in nature. In true food allergy, the body produces IgE antibodies in response to the food allergen. When IgE antibodies are not present, the reaction is food intolerance. For example, some people who experience stomach cramping and diarrhea after drinking milk are lacking an enzyme called lactase. Lactase helps to digest the lactose (a sugar) in milk. IgE antibodies are not present in this reaction, so it is an intolerance, not an allergy. Some people experience an adverse reaction to food additives, such as aspartame (a calorie-free sweetener) and monosodium glutamate (a flavor enhancer also known as MSG). They might have stomach cramps or nausea after eating these substances.

About 3 percent of children and about 1 percent of adults have true food allergies. Although food allergies usually develop during infancy or childhood, they can develop at any age. People can develop reactions to foods that they have eaten for many years without a problem. Food allergies can be very difficult to diagnose and treat. Medications and immunotherapy are not effective in food allergies. The only way to avoid reactions is to stay away from the foods that cause them.

FOODS THAT CAUSE ALLERGIC REACTIONS

Almost any food can cause an allergic reaction in someone. But some foods seem to cause problems for more people than others. The most common food allergens are cow's milk, eggs, fish and shellfish, nuts, grains, and legumes, which include peas, beans, and peanuts.

Most of the foods on the list of common allergens are the foods we eat every day. Most people can eat as much of these foods as often as they please. For the people who are allergic, eating these foods causes discomfort and much worse.

MILK

Milk has several different proteins that can produce an allergic reaction in people who are allergic to it. Avoiding these proteins is often difficult because they are found in so many foods. Cheese, yogurt, ice cream, pudding, butter, some breads and pastries, and even some candies are made with milk. Milk products are even put in some processed meats, such as luncheon meat and hot dogs. The allergic symptoms that milk proteins cause include skin rash, stuffy nose, wheezing, nausea, and vomiting. Anaphylaxis also can occur.

Milk and milk products, including cheese, can cause allergic reactions. Milk allergy is the most common childhood allergy.

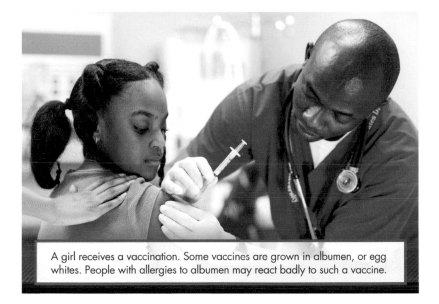

A girl receives a vaccination. Some vaccines are grown in albumen, or egg whites. People with allergies to albumen may react badly to such a vaccine.

EGGS

The white of the egg, not the yolk, causes trouble for people who are allergic to eggs. The white of the egg contains a protein called albumin, which is highly allergenic. Avoiding the whites is practically impossible because in separating an egg, some of the white usually slips in with the yolk. Because of this, people who are allergic to eggs have to avoid foods even when the label lists egg yolks as an ingredient.

Symptoms of an allergic reaction to eggs include skin rash or hives, swelling, nausea, vomiting, and anaphylaxis. As they grow older, children who are allergic to eggs may become more tolerant of them. However, this allergy may continue into adulthood. Some vaccines, such as the MMR (measles, mumps, and rubella) vaccine given to children and flu shots given to teenagers and adults, may cause a strong reaction in people allergic to eggs because the vaccines are grown in chicken eggs. Interestingly, being allergic to eggs does not

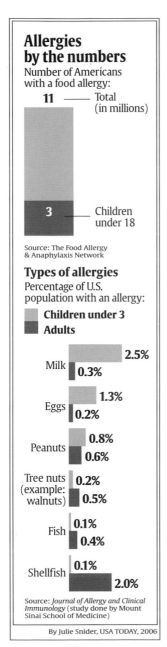

Allergies by the numbers

Number of Americans with a food allergy:

11 —— Total (in millions)

3 —— Children under 18

Source: The Food Allergy & Anaphylaxis Network

Types of allergies

Percentage of U.S. population with an allergy:

■ **Children under 3**
■ **Adults**

Milk
2.5%
0.3%

Eggs
1.3%
0.2%

Peanuts
0.8%
0.6%

Tree nuts (example: walnuts)
0.2%
0.5%

Fish
0.1%
0.4%

Shellfish
0.1%
2.0%

Source: *Journal of Allergy and Clinical Immunology* (study done by Mount Sinai School of Medicine)

By Julie Snider, USA TODAY, 2006

carry over to chicken meat. Someone who is allergic to eggs could be allergic to chicken, but not because of being allergic to eggs. One allergy has nothing to do with the other.

FISH AND SHELLFISH

Tuna, salmon, and catfish are called bony fishes. Crabs, lobsters, shrimp, clams, oysters, scallops, and mussels are shellfish. People who are allergic to one type of bony fish are likely to be allergic to all types of bony fish. And people who are allergic to one type of shellfish are likely to be allergic to all types of shellfish. Some people are allergic to both bony fish and shellfish.

Allergic reactions to fish and shellfish can be severe. Symptoms include rash, hives, and swelling, or anaphylaxis. Some very sensitive people actually experience coughing and wheezing when they breathe the odor of fish or shellfish cooking on the stove.

TREE NUTS

Tree nuts include walnuts, almonds, pecans, hazelnuts, and Brazil nuts. The most common symptoms of an allergic reaction to tree nuts are hives and anaphylaxis. However, some reactions are not as severe and involve only stomach discomfort. The most difficult aspect of nut allergy is that nuts are hard to avoid. They are widely used as an ingredient in other products. Even some salad dressings contain nuts as an ingredient.

GRAINS

Although wheat allergy is most common among children, some adults suffer from it as well. The symptoms of a reaction include a rash and sometimes wheezing, coughing, and hives. Wheat is found in breads and other baked goods, cereals, pasta, and even some soups. Processed

Eggs, milk, grain, shellfish, legumes, and soy beans are among common food allergens.

meats, such as hamburgers and hot dogs, sometimes contain wheat.

Oats, corn, rye, and rice are other grains that can cause allergic reactions in some people. They, too, are often contained in other products. The most common symptoms of this allergy are bloating, diarrhea, and constipation.

LEGUMES

Peanuts are a legume, not a nut. The legume family also includes peas and beans, such as garbanzo, navy, and pinto beans. These beans are round or oval and have pasty insides, similar to peas. Soybeans, black-eyed peas, and lentils also belong to this group.

String beans and green beans are not legumes. Licorice is a legume as well.

Of the legumes, soybeans and peanuts most commonly cause allergic reactions. It is the beans themselves that cause a reaction because the beans contain protein. Peanut protein is one of the most potent of all allergens. Allergic reactions to peanuts often involve anaphylaxis. Many foods, such as some breads, crackers, cereals, processed meats, salad dressings, and soups contain soybean products. Even candy and ice cream may contain soybeans.

When peanut oil and soybean oil are very pure, they contain no protein and will not cause an allergic reaction. But during processing, some of the protein often slips into the oil as the beans are pressed. Oil that contains even a trace amount of protein can cause a reaction in people who are highly sensitive.

SYMPTOMS

Before you can have an allergic reaction to a food, you must be sensitized to that particular food. You will have to eat the food at least once before your body can recognize it as an allergen. Sensitization can take place very early in life. Some doctors believe that infants can become sensitized through their mothers' milk. If a nursing mother frequently eats eggs, for example, her baby may become sensitized to eggs even before he or she actually eats eggs.

Once your body becomes sensitized, a reaction will begin and symptoms will appear within a few minutes or as long as four hours after you eat the food. The first part of the body to react is often the mouth, where itching may begin. As the body digests the food, abdominal pain, vomiting, and diarrhea may occur. Even the nose and skin may react—the nose runs and the skin breaks out in a rash or hives.

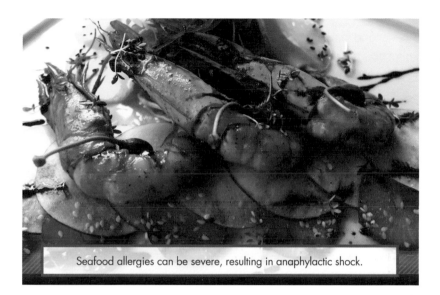

Seafood allergies can be severe, resulting in anaphylactic shock.

The severity of the reaction varies from person to person. Some experience mild symptoms. They may get the sniffles or a mild rash after eating a certain food. But others experience severe reactions with life-threatening symptoms, such as swelling of the tongue, throat, or bronchi of the lungs.

Allergic reactions to food can be unpredictable. They might change depending on the quantity eaten and the amount of time that has passed since eating the food. Someone who is allergic to corn may experience only bloating and no other symptoms after eating it, as long as small portions are eaten only occasionally. But when larger portions are eaten more frequently, the symptoms become more severe.

Some people react to a certain food allergen with consistent, specific symptoms. Their symptoms will always be the same, no matter how much of the food they have eaten or how much time has passed since they last ate it. Another person who is allergic to corn, for example, will react with stomach cramps after eating food containing corn. That person will react this way no matter how much of the food has been eaten or how often. Anyone who has had an anaphylactic reaction must strictly avoid the offending food, however. Just a tiny amount can cause a life-threatening reaction, even if the food has not been eaten for a very long time. The individual should carry an EpiPen and wear a medical emergency tag.

In people whose food allergy appears before the age of three, symptoms sometimes diminish or disappear later in life. Milk and egg allergies that show up very early in life are most commonly associated with fading symptoms. This means that young children who are allergic to milk or eggs and develop a rash when they ingest them may not develop a rash later in life. As adults, they may be able to ingest milk or eggs without developing any reaction. Symptoms of peanut, tree nut, and fish and shellfish allergies, on the other hand, tend to remain noticeable for a lifetime. Reactions often are severe.

DIAGNOSIS

Diagnosing a food allergy can be simple. A reaction that occurs within a few minutes of eating a certain food is a fairly good indicator that food allergy exists and of which food caused the allergic reaction. But sometimes it can be difficult to determine the culprit food. The doctor will have to rely on information from you. Your doctor may ask:

- What symptoms were involved during the reaction?
- How long after the food was eaten did symptoms appear?
- Have you had a reaction at other times after eating this food?
- How much of the food had you eaten at the time the reaction occurred?
- Had you also eaten other foods before the reaction began?
- Did anyone else have a reaction, such as nausea, vomiting, or diarrhea, after eating the same food?

www.usatoday.com

USA TODAY

Life

SECTION D

December 7, 2010

From the Pages of USA TODAY

Finally, guidance on food allergies; Doctors urged to be thorough in diagnosis

Doctors should take a thorough medical history when they suspect a patient might have a food allergy, according to the first-ever clinical guidelines for diagnosing and managing such allergies.

Food allergies afflict 5% of children and 4% of adults in the USA—10 million to 12 million people—and appear to be on the rise, says the National Institute of Allergy and Infectious Diseases, which developed the standards.

Allergic reactions to certain foods, including eggs, dairy, wheat and peanuts, can be severe, even deadly, and there are no cures. Peanut allergies in particular appear to be increasing, says Matthew Fenton, chief of the Asthma, Allergy and Inflammation Branch of the Division of Allergy, Immunology and Transplantation at the allergy institute.

More than 30 professional organizations, agencies and patient advocacy groups were involved in developing the guidelines.

A summary appears in the *Journal of Allergy and Clinical Immunology*, and the full report is available at jacionline.org. Fenton says the institute plans to publish a synopsis of the guidelines for parents.

Fenton says he's "very hopeful we're going to see similar strides in diagnosis and treatment of food allergies that we saw after the introduction of asthma guidelines years ago."

The guidelines stress the importance of a thorough medical history, and they include a list of the most useful tests to determine the nature of the allergy.

The guidelines include:

- The definition of a food allergy and allergens, as well as food-induced conditions such as anaphylaxis, a life-threatening symptom.
- Foods that commonly cause reactions, including tree nuts and seafood.
- Symptoms, including skin reactions and breathing and gastrointestinal problems.
- Diagnostic guidelines, including when food allergy should be suspected and tests conducted.
- Tests and combinations of tests that are useful and not useful in determining certain types of food allergies.
- Management of disease, depending on type of allergy.

—*Mary Brophy Marcus*

The doctor may conclude that the reaction was caused by bacteria in the food and not food allergy. But if the doctor does suspect food allergy, a skin test can confirm the diagnosis. A blood test can determine the presence of IgE antibodies to specific food allergens.

TREATMENT

Your doctor may prescribe an antihistamine or an oral corticosteroid to relieve your symptoms. These medications cannot prevent a reaction from taking place. But they can help when a reaction is already under way.

Avoidance is the key to dealing with food allergy. Once you have discovered what food or foods you are allergic to, avoid them completely. Some people are so highly allergic that eating just one tiny bite of the culprit food could cause anaphylaxis. Just a piece of a peanut in a cookie or a single spoonful of clam chowder could cause death. Packaged foods that you buy at the grocery store include a list of ingredients on the box or the wrapper. If you train yourself to be regular and thorough about reading labels, you should be able to avoid the foods that cause problems. Perhaps have someone else double-check the label for you.

Don't be surprised to find that the most unlikely foods contain things that you are allergic to. Did you know that some store-bought bread crumbs contain sesame seeds? Or that some sherbets contain egg whites? Did you know that a brand of cheese spread on the market contains anchovies, a type of small bony fish? The anchovies help give this cheese spread its unique flavor.

Accidents sometimes happen, no matter how careful you are. Some seemingly innocent foods can end up being problem foods. And occasionally, the labels on foods are inaccurate. So even if you have read the label and the culprit food is not listed, it may be in the food product anyway. An example is a name-brand cookie dough ice cream sold in supermarkets that the manufacturer recalled because the label on the container did not list eggs as one of the ingredients in the cookie dough. People with severe food allergies should always have an emergency kit available with a syringe of epinephrine and antihistamine tablets.

For kids with food allergies, school lunches can be dangerous. Allergens could be in foods without being visible.

Eating in restaurants is difficult if you have food allergies, especially if your reactions are severe. Even eating in the school cafeteria can be a problem. You do not have control over the food preparation or what foods get near other foods. If you are allergic to sesame seeds, can you be sure a sesame seed from a sandwich bun has not dropped into your salad? If you are allergic to shellfish, can you be sure your french fries were not fried in the same oil as someone else's fried shrimp? Dining out can be risky, but that doesn't mean you can never eat at a restaurant. Just ask your server to confirm with the kitchen that your order does not include any foods that you cannot eat. Most restaurants have experience with this and their staff is trained to help customers with allergies.

CHAPTER SIX

DRUG ALLERGIES

KELLY'S STORY

I had strep throat (a sore throat caused by streptococcal bacteria), and my doctor prescribed penicillin, which I had taken several times before. After taking the medicine for two days, I actually felt worse than I did before I started taking it. My parents told me it would just take time, so I kept taking it. But on the fifth night, my fever was up to 103 degrees and I had an itchy rash on my stomach and pain in my joints. It hurt too much to even walk.

My parents called the doctor, and he said it was a reaction to the penicillin. He told me to stop taking the medication immediately. The fever went away the next day and the rash disappeared, but I had the joint pain for almost a month. I was hobbling through the halls at school and friends had to help me carry my books. I couldn't participate in gym, either. It was horrible.

I can't take any medicine with penicillin in it anymore. We had to notify the pharmacy and my dentist and dermatologist.

Suppose your doctor prescribes an antibiotic to treat your sore throat. You are directed to take one capsule three times a day for seven days. On the first day, you feel queasy from the medication, but you have no other symptoms. Your doctor tells you that this is an adverse reaction and instructs you to continue taking the medication for the full seven days.

Suppose your doctor prescribes an antibiotic for your sore throat and you do well on the first day, but on the second day, you develop itchy hives all over your body. The doctor tells you that this is an indication of an allergic reaction and that you should stop taking the medication. The doctor then prescribes a different antibiotic for you.

Drugs can cause both adverse reactions and allergic reactions. The difference is that an adverse reaction may cause unpleasant symptoms, but the body does not respond by producing IgE antibodies. Furthermore, an adverse reaction can occur the first time you swallow or are injected with a drug, unlike an allergic reaction.

An allergic reaction occurs only after you are sensitized to a drug. But sensitization sometimes takes place very quickly. It can occur after just one or two doses of a drug. And sometimes the first exposure to a drug can happen when a person is too young to remember it later in life—perhaps through milk a baby gets from its mother.

DRUGS THAT CAUSE ALLERGIC REACTIONS

Almost any drug can cause an allergic reaction. Penicillin, an antibiotic used to treat infections, tops the list. People like Kelly

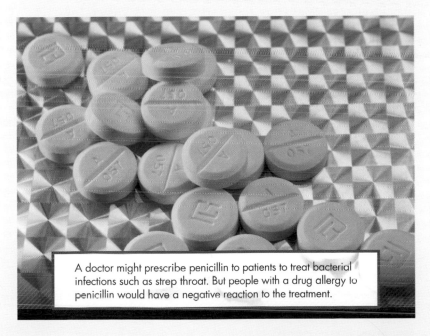

A doctor might prescribe penicillin to patients to treat bacterial infections such as strep throat. But people with a drug allergy to penicillin would have a negative reaction to the treatment.

who are allergic to penicillin must beware of other antibiotics in the same family, such as ampicillin and amoxicillin. Furthermore, people who are allergic to one antibiotic are at risk for having an allergic reaction to other antibiotics. This is true even if the antibiotics are not in the same family. Other drugs known to cause allergic reactions are sulfa drugs (antibiotics that contain sulfonamides), insulin, seizure medications, and anesthetics.

Someone may take a drug for weeks, months, or even years without having an allergic reaction and then suddenly suffer a severe reaction. For that person, the slightest exposure in the future will cause allergic symptoms.

SYMPTOMS

Most allergic reactions to drugs are mild and appear as an itchy rash or hives on the skin. But reactions to drugs can be severe and may involve swelling (lips, tongue, throat, eyes, fingers, or hands), runny nose, wheezing, nausea, and vomiting. Typically, the more rapidly symptoms appear, the more dangerous the reaction is. A reaction that occurs within minutes to an hour after taking the drug can be life threatening. This can occur with penicillin and with anesthetics—both local, which numb one area of the body (novocaine, for example), and general, which affect the entire body. Injectable drugs are more likely to cause anaphylaxis than those taken orally in tablet, capsule, or liquid form. Penicillin can be taken orally or by injection. The rate of anaphylaxis is higher when penicillin is injected.

An adverse reaction can be as unpleasant as an allergic reaction, although it is not life threatening. Symptoms can continue for hours, days, or even weeks after taking the drug. These symptoms may involve a rash (often not itchy), lumps under the skin, and black-

and-blue marks. An adverse reaction also can cause blood, liver, and kidney problems. In some cases, even the lymph glands and joints become swollen and tender, and there may be fever. Kelly's reaction to penicillin involved these symptoms in addition to the symptoms of an allergic reaction.

DIAGNOSIS

The diagnosis of drug allergy is often difficult. Doctors often suggest that their patients stop taking a prescribed drug if a reaction occurs, just to be on the safe side. And if you stop taking the drug in question and the symptoms disappear relatively quickly, the problem is probably an allergy. Doctors rely on patient history to make a diagnosis.

Skin tests and blood tests such as RAST have not proven very useful to doctors in diagnosing drug allergies. But an elevated count of eosinophils in a routine blood test can help confirm a drug allergy.

The only way to test whether a drug is actually causing an allergic reaction is to rechallenge the person with the suspected drug. A drug challenge usually is used only when an emergency arises and the particular drug is needed. In a drug challenge, the person takes the same drug again to see if a reaction occurs. This must be done under a doctor's supervision and after all symptoms from the previous reaction are gone.

TREATMENT

A severe reaction, such as anaphylaxis, should be treated with an immediate injection of epinephrine. For a less severe reaction, the doctor may suggest the use of antihistamines and topical corticosteroid creams to help relieve symptoms.

www.usatoday.com

USA TODAY

Life

SECTION D

March 9, 2009

From the Pages of USA TODAY

Many think they have drug allergies; When those drugs just might be the best medicine

Are you allergic to any medicines? It's one of those basic questions we get (or should get) every time we see a new doctor, check in for a medical procedure or enter an emergency room.

And, doctors say, it's a question people routinely answer incorrectly—usually by claiming an allergy to a drug that actually is safe for them.

"It's an extremely common scenario," says David Khan, director of allergy and immunology training at the University of Texas Southwestern Medical Center. And it's an expensive, troublesome one, since common drugs people believe are dangerous for them—ranging from penicillin to aspirin—often are the cheapest, best drugs for their illnesses.

The problem was illustrated in a study published in February in the *Annals of Emergency Medicine*. Researchers in a Cincinnati [Ohio] emergency department used a skin test to check for penicillin allergy in 150 patients who said they were allergic to the drug. Only 13 tested positive, meaning more than 90% could almost certainly take penicillin and related drugs without risking a dangerous reaction.

Many penicillin studies have found similar results, say researchers Jonathan Bernstein, an allergist and immunologist, and Joseph Moellman, an emergency physician. Both teach at the University of Cincinnati College of Medicine.

But the problem goes beyond penicillin. Allergists see patients every day who

Anyone who has experienced an allergic reaction to a drug should wear a medical emergency tag even if the reaction was mild. Being exposed to the drug the next time could cause a more severe reaction. The best treatment for drug allergy is to stop taking the offending drug and avoid taking it in the future.

are wrongly convinced they have drug allergies, say Khan, Bernstein and Stuart Friedman, an allergist and immunologist in Delray Beach, Fla. Among the explanations:

People confuse unpleasant side effects with allergic reactions. For example, lots of people get upset stomachs when they take aspirin.

People trust their mothers, who say they had reactions as children. But often the reaction was a rash caused by an illness, not a drug.

People trust their doctors. Often, people having possible allergic reactions call their doctors and are told to stop taking drugs—but are never examined or questioned in detail to find out whether their problems really were allergic reactions.

People grow out of some allergies.

The solution is not for patients to stop telling doctors about suspected drug allergies; the information is potentially lifesaving. But doctors could correct a lot of records by taking more detailed histories and by sending patients with hard-to-interpret stories to allergy specialists, experts say.

An allergist often can rule out an aller-gy by giving patients gradually increased doses of the suspect medication, Khan says. And, sometimes, patients who are truly allergic to a needed drug can safely get gradually increased doses under strict, well-tested protocols, he says.

Quick allergy skin testing is not workable or available for drugs other than penicillin, mostly for technical reasons. And even penicillin skin tests, used for decades, are not widely available, because the only commercial version was pulled off the market by the Food and Drug Administration [FDA] in 2004, because of manufacturing concerns. A company called AllerQuest is working with the FDA to return the test kit to the market, says company founder Louis Mendelson, a Connecticut allergist.

Widespread penicillin allergy testing could reduce the use of antibiotics that are more likely to spur the growth of drug-resistant germs, Moellman says. The Cincinnati study was the first to show testing could work in an emergency department. The researchers used a test kit made in their own lab and did not receive funding from any company.

—Kim Painter

If your doctor has diagnosed you with a drug allergy, you should mention this to any doctor you go to afterward. You should always tell a new doctor about your allergy in case the doctor prescribes a medication. Learn which other drugs are in the same family as the drug that caused the reaction. You should avoid the entire family of

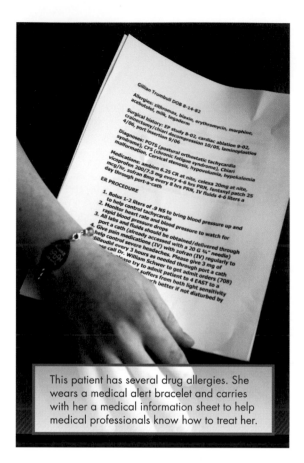

Gillian Trumbull DOB 8-14-82

Allergies: zithromax, biaxin, erythromycin, morphine, acebutolol, milk, tegaderm

Surgical history: EP study 8-02, cardiac ablation 9-02, craniectomy/Chiari decompression 10/05, laminoplasties 4/06, port insertion 9/06

Diagnoses: POTS (postural orthostatic tachycardia syndrome), CFS (chronic fatigue syndrome), Chiari malformation, Cervical stenosis, hypovolumia, hypokalemia

Medications: ambien 6.25 CR at nite, celexa 20mg at nite, vicoprofen 200/7.5 mg every 4-6 hrs PRN, fentanyl patch 25 mcg/hr, zofran 8mg every 8 hrs PRN, IV fluids 4-6 liters a day through port-a-cath

ER PROCEDURE

1. Bolus 1-2 liters of .9 NS to bring blood pressure up and to help control tachycardia
2. Monitor heart rate and blood pressure to watch for rapid blood pressure drops
3. All labs and fluids should be obtained/delivered through port a cath (already accessed with a 20 G ¾" needle)
4. Give pain medications (IV) with zofran (IV) regularly to help control severe headaches. Please give 3 mg of dilaudid every 3 hours as needed through port a cath …se call Dr. William Schwer to get admit orders (708) … try to admit patient to 4 EAST to a … suffers from both light sensitivity … better if not disturbed by

This patient has several drug allergies. She wears a medical alert bracelet and carries with her a medical information sheet to help medical professionals know how to treat her.

drugs. Many pharmacies keep information about each customer on file. That way, when filling a prescription, the pharmacist can advise whether it is safe to take the drug or whether it belongs to a group of drugs that should be avoided.

Someone who has developed an allergy to one drug is at risk for developing an allergy to other drugs. For this reason, take medications only when absolutely necessary. Taking medications at times when an illness might clear up on its own could cause sensitization to a drug that might later be needed to treat a serious illness. A good example is overuse of antibiotics. Antibiotics attack bacteria, not viruses. If you take them for viral infections, your body may become unnecessarily sensitized. The antibiotic then cannot be used to tackle a bacterial infection if it should arise. And sometimes a particular antibiotic is better than all others in fighting a certain type of infection. But if you have been sensitized to the antibiotic and have become allergic, it cannot be used to treat your infection. Even overuse of an antibiotic ointment can sensitize you to the antibiotics contained in the ointment. Sensitization often does not occur until you have taken a medication several times. You can put off becoming sensitized by not taking medications when not needed.

CHAPTER SEVEN

INSECT ALLERGIES

AARON'S STORY

I run track, and the field is behind our school. One day during practice, I went over to the bleachers to cool off. I poured some water over my head and then dried my face with a towel, and I got stung on the cheek. The insect must have been stuck in my towel. I didn't think much of it because I've been stung before, but when I went back to the track, I didn't feel well. I felt itchy and sick to my stomach. I could feel the side of my face start to swell, and I could hardly talk. My coach noticed something was wrong, and he started walking toward me. Everything was spinning, and I felt as if I was going to faint. I told him I had been stung, and he made me sit down. He called 911 on his cell phone, and by the time the ambulance came, I felt as if I had a boulder on my chest. I just couldn't inhale the air. They rushed me to the hospital, and the doctor gave me two shots, which helped a lot.

We weren't sure what had stung me. I thought it was a bee, but the doctor told me it could have been a wasp or a hornet. My dad went back to the track field to check around the bleachers for a nest. He found a wasps' nest in a corner of the bleachers, so we thought maybe I had been stung by a wasp.

Later, we met with an allergist, and he gave me a blood test, which showed that I'm allergic to wasp venom. He recommended that I get allergy shots twice a week, and that's supposed to help me be less sensitive to wasp stings. I also keep an emergency insect-sting kit with me when I'm outdoors, and I wear an emergency medical tag. I still run track, but I'm more careful now.

Have you ever been stung by a bee or a wasp? Were you left with a small, red raised area at the site of the sting? Was there even a little pain? Did the discomfort then disappear within a few hours or days? If you answered "yes" to these questions, you have had the reaction most people have when they are stung. But for people who are allergic, being stung is far more serious. An allergic reaction to an insect sting can even cause death.

STINGING INSECTS THAT CAUSE ALLERGIC REACTIONS

In the United States, the stinging insects that cause serious allergic reactions are honeybees, bumblebees, wasps, hornets, yellow jackets, and fire ants. Honeybees and bumblebees belong to one family of insects. Hornets, wasps, and yellow jackets belong to a second. Fire ants belong to a third.

Each stinging insect attacks its victim a bit differently. Honeybees sting only once and then go off to die. They have barbed stingers that get stuck in the victim's flesh. The honeybee's venom sac is attached to the end of the stinger. While the stinger is embedded in skin, it

A close-up photo of the back end of a bee shows its stinger. Bee stings are always painful. For a person allergic to bee venom, they can be deadly.

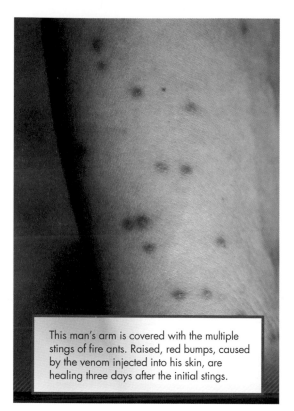
This man's arm is covered with the multiple stings of fire ants. Raised, red bumps, caused by the venom injected into his skin, are healing three days after the initial stings.

releases venom into the person's body. Hornets, wasps, and yellow jackets do not have barbs on their stingers. Since their stingers do not get stuck in the flesh, these insects are able to sting their victims several times, pumping venom into the flesh with each sting. A fire ant bites into its victim with its mandibles (like jaws). While holding on, the ant pivots around and stings with the stinger on the rear of its body. Fire ants can also sting repeatedly.

The venom from these stinging insects causes the allergic reaction. Some of the chemicals that make up the venom are toxic, or poisonous. This is what causes the pain and small red bump that most people experience after being stung. Everyone reacts negatively to the toxicity of the venom. In fact, someone who is stung several hundred times by yellow jackets, for example, risks death from a reaction to the toxicity of the venom and not from an allergic reaction to it.

But other chemicals are also in the venom, and these cause an allergic reaction. They are the allergens, and they cause histamine to be released in people who are allergic. The chemicals that make up the venom vary from species to species. Related insects (those in the same family) all have venom similar enough to cause a reaction in someone who is allergic. For example, if you are allergic to the venom of yellow jackets, you also may be allergic to the venom of hornets and wasps.

SYMPTOMS

An allergic reaction to an insect sting often begins with itching around the eyes and mouth, followed by flushing of the skin and a slight cough. In some people, the reaction stops there. In others, an entire arm or leg might swell. In still others, the reaction rapidly progresses. It may go on to cause an outbreak of itchy hives, swelling of the throat, tightness in the chest, nausea and vomiting, shortness of breath, dizziness, and a feeling of enveloping doom. Some even lose consciousness and die. All of this can happen in less than thirty minutes and from just one sting.

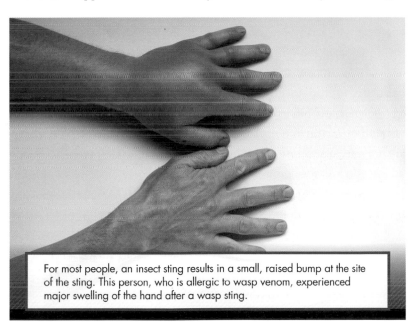

For most people, an insect sting results in a small, raised bump at the site of the sting. This person, who is allergic to wasp venom, experienced major swelling of the hand after a wasp sting.

An allergic reaction cannot occur before sensitization has taken place. You will not experience the symptoms of a reaction the first time you are stung. You may have a reaction after you are stung a second time or maybe even later.

Sometimes it can be quite a while between the sensitization and the symptoms of an allergic reaction. For example, suppose you were stung by a yellow jacket when you were five years old. A painful red bump developed but disappeared within a few hours. The next time you were stung, at eleven, your skin became flushed, you started to cough, and your entire arm swelled. The first sting sensitized you to yellow jacket venom. Then, six years later, a sting caused an allergic reaction.

DIAGNOSIS

To find out which insect you are allergic to, collect the one that stung you and take it to your doctor for analysis. If that is not possible, the doctor will look for telltale signs of a specific insect. Honeybees' barbed stingers remain in your flesh after a sting. Fire ants leave a pattern of multiple stings. When these signs are not present, doctors use other methods of identification. The doctor will ask you to remember as much about the incident as you can: what the insect looked like, how it moved, the time of day the sting occurred, and where you were when it happened.

Stinging insects have distinct body shapes or markings and certain habits. Bumblebees are large and fat, with yellow and black stripes. Honeybees are smaller, with rounded yellow or brownish bodies. The bodies of yellow jackets, hornets, and wasps are narrow in the middle, as if they have waists.

Yellow jackets are thin, with yellow and black stripes. They love sweet food and often are found around picnic areas and garbage

If you have an insect allergy, be sure to know which species of stinging insect you are allergic to so you can avoid the insects and the places they live.

cans. They usually nest in or near the ground. If you disturb a yellow jacket nest while you are mowing the lawn or playing a sport, they will attack in a swarm.

Hornets have yellow or white stripes and white faces. They are known for their large cone-shaped nests. The nests hang from trees or under the eaves of a house.

Wasps are brown or black and usually build their nests on or near a house. They are most likely to sting when disturbed. They also tend to hide in clothing and shoes and will sting if disturbed, as Aaron learned.

Fire ants live in the southern part of the United States and are found from Florida to Texas. They have wings, but they do not fly. They crawl on the ground and build their nests there. Their sting feels like a minor burn, which is how they got their name.

After the doctor gathers as much information as possible from talking to you, skin or blood tests can confirm a diagnosis. Skin testing is done with venom from the various stinging insects. But it cannot be done until at least six weeks after you were stung. Your body needs time to replenish the supply of IgE antibodies that were used up during the allergic reaction. Blood testing also may be done. A blood sample is sent to a laboratory. There, a technician mixes it with some specially prepared venom from the suspected insect. The presence of IgE antibodies indicates an allergy to that venom.

TREATMENT

There are things you can do and medications you can take to help relieve the symptoms of an insect sting. As with food allergies, people who are allergic to insect stings should always carry an emergency kit. They should wear a medical alert bracelet in case of emergencies. For less severe reactions, the following steps can help:

Remove the stinger. If the stinger is embedded in the skin, scrape it out immediately with your fingernail. Tweezers or any other object that would squeeze the stinger should not be used because more venom could be forced from the sac into the sting site. Scraping out the stinger is best. By removing the stinger with your fingernail, the amount of venom that goes into the blood is kept as low as possible.

Use meat tenderizer. Make a paste of meat tenderizer and water and apply it to the affected area within the first few minutes after the sting. This reduces pain and swelling. This will help only with a local reaction, such as on the hand or foot. It will not help with a systemic reaction (one that involves the entire body).

Take medications. If the reaction is more severe, you can get a prescription for a corticosteroid cream to apply to the sting site. The doctor also may suggest that you use antihistamines to help relieve itching and inflammation. The sting site must

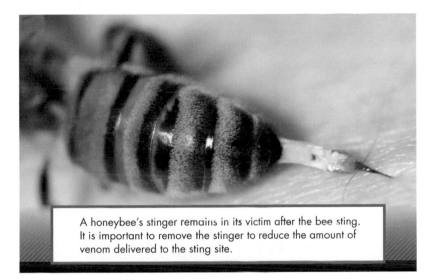

A honeybee's stinger remains in its victim after the bee sting. It is important to remove the stinger to reduce the amount of venom delivered to the sting site.

be kept clean to avoid infection. You can wash it with soap and water. Be careful not to break any blister that may have formed on your skin.

A severe reaction, such as one that involves widespread hives, wheezing, and loss of consciousness, should be treated as an emergency. An injection of epinephrine is needed to reverse the allergic reaction. The victim should be taken immediately to the nearest hospital.

Use a tourniquet. A tourniquet, a device wrapped tightly around an arm or a leg, usually to control bleeding, can help keep the venom from spreading through your body. If the sting is on your hand, arm, foot, or leg, for example, you can apply a tourniquet above the sting site to keep the venom from spreading further through your body. Loosen the tourniquet for one minute every three minutes so that the blood supply is not completely cut off. Elevate the affected area and apply ice or a cold pack to reduce the pain and swelling. The cold pack also will help slow down the spread of the venom.

Immunotherapy. Allergy shots, or immunotherapy, can also help. Doctors usually use this treatment only if you have had a reaction involving the entire body. The shots help you build up a tolerance for the venom. Someone could be allergic to more than one insect from the group. So doctors sometimes use mixed-venom extracts in the allergy shots.

A doctor will give you shots with specially prepared venom twice a week for the first few months. The doctor will then gradually increase the dose until a maintenance dose is set. Then the injections can be given less frequently, such as every four to six weeks. Usually allergy shots continue for about five years. But some people must continue them for life. One type of allergy shot is not from venom. Fire ant allergy shots are an extract of the bodies of the insects because both the venom and the body proteins are allergenic.

Desensitization by immunotherapy can reduce the risk of life-threatening reactions to insect stings. Anyone who has had an anaphylactic reaction to a sting should still carry an emergency kit because the allergy shots may not provide full protection.

PREVENTION

Avoiding being stung is the best way to deal with stinging insects, especially if you are at risk for severe reactions. Here are some things you can do to protect yourself:

- Stay away from garbage cans, especially ones without lids.
- Wear closed shoes rather than sandals when you are outdoors. Never walk barefoot.
- Cover as much of your body with clothing as possible. Wear muted colors such as white, green, tan, beige, or khaki. Avoid brightly colored, floral-printed, and dark-colored clothing.

- Avoid extremely loose-fitting clothing that would allow insects to get between the fabric and your skin.
- Do not wear shiny jewelry.
- Do not wear perfume, cologne, or other scented cosmetics, such as lotions or hair products.
- Avoid eating outdoors. If you do eat outdoors, do not drink from cans or bottles because insects may be inside.
- Do not touch, pick up, step on, or sit on anything outdoors before first checking for insects.
- If an insect gets into the car while you are driving, pull off the road, open all the windows, and leave the car until the insect flies away. Do not swat at it or make any noise. Always keep the windows closed when the car is parked.
- If you are outdoors and an attack by an insect or a group of insects seems unavoidable, move away slowly. Make no sudden movements. Do not flail your arms or swat at them.

BITING INSECTS THAT CAUSE ALLERGIC REACTIONS

Stinging insects are not the only ones that cause allergic reactions. Biting insects also cause reactions in people who are allergic to them. Some of the biting insects include mosquitoes, biting flies, kissing bugs, fleas, and bedbugs. The best way to deal with these insects is to avoid being bitten. Insecticides and insect repellents can help.

Most of us have experienced the pain of being bitten by mosquitoes. The red bumps that are left behind cause discomfort afterward because of their intense itch. People who are allergic experience an exaggerated reaction. A few hours after being bitten, they experience swelling and more intense itching. An oral antihistamine often helps. In some cases, the reaction can even involve hives, dizziness, and nausea.

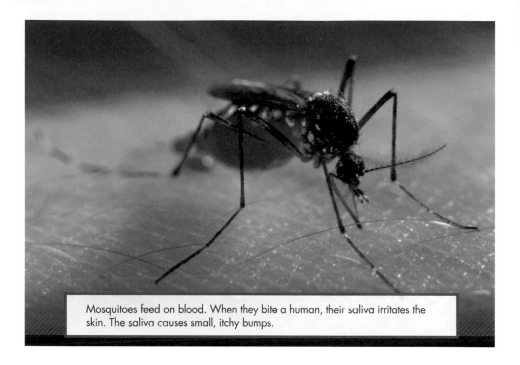

Mosquitoes feed on blood. When they bite a human, their saliva irritates the skin. The saliva causes small, itchy bumps.

Deerflies, blackflies, horseflies, and biting midge flies are the most common culprits that cause allergic reactions. Biting flies are more likely to cause an allergic reaction than mosquitoes. Deerfly and horsefly bites tend to be painful. Blackfly bites can cause swelling. Biting midge fly bites tend to cause both pain and swelling. They also can cause itching. In people who are especially sensitive, the bites of biting flies can cause anaphylaxis. Allergy shots can help some but not all of these individuals.

Kissing bugs tend to attack while their victims sleep. Their name comes from their preference for biting the face. Kissing bug bites are usually painless, but allergic reactions can be severe. Allergy shots for these bites are effective.

Flea bites can cause groups of itchy skin eruptions on people who are allergic. Red or brownish hives tend to break out on the arms, legs, the face, and the neck, or the shoulder and hips. Allergy shots for flea bites are not effective and can even create greater sensitivity. Topical corticosteroid creams and antihistamines can relieve the itching.

A bedbug's bite is not painful because it injects an anesthetic substance into its victim while it is biting it. It leaves behind lines of reddish bumps on the skin. People who are especially sensitive experience widespread hives, shortness of breath, and joint pain. Topical corticosteroid creams

A bedbug bites a person's skin. Bedbugs have become a big problem in some major cities around the world.

and antihistamines relieve the itching. Oral corticosteroids reduce inflammation.

CHAPTER EIGHT

ASTHMA

MELISSA'S STORY

One day when my mom was vacuuming, I suddenly started to feel as if I couldn't catch my breath. I went to my room and lay down on my bed, thinking that I would have an easier time breathing if I just rested. But it didn't help. I felt scared, because it had never happened before.

That night at the dinner table, my mom got a funny look on her face and said, "Stop doing that, Melissa." I didn't know what she was talking about. When I asked her what I was doing, she said, "You're making that funny sound. Please stop fooling around at the dinner table." I realized that I was making a whistling sound when I breathed, and I wasn't doing it on purpose. I started to cry, which just made everything worse. My mom knew I wasn't fooling around. I explained to her what had happened in the morning when she was vacuuming. She thought I was probably coming down with a cold.

The next day at school, I was having trouble breathing, and this time my chest felt very tight, like someone was squeezing it. I knew it wasn't a cold, but I didn't know what was wrong with me. I went to the nurse, and she called my mom. She told my mom to take me straight to the doctor's office because she thought I might be having an asthma episode. My doctor examined me and gave me some medicine, and I felt a little better. He referred us to an asthma specialist.

The asthma specialist asked me a lot of questions and gave me some breathing tests. She said she thought my problem was asthma, and she felt that an allergy to dust and dust mites could be triggering my symptoms. She did a scratch test for dust and dust mites, and I started wheezing. The doctor said this confirmed the diagnosis.

The doctor prescribed medication for me to take every day to prevent an asthma episode from starting, and she prescribed other medication I can take if an episode starts. She also recommended some changes we could make around our house to cut down on the amount of dust and dust mites.

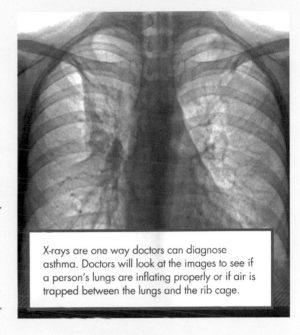

X-rays are one way doctors can diagnose asthma. Doctors will look at the images to see if a person's lungs are inflating properly or if air is trapped between the lungs and the rib cage.

My dad pulled up all the carpeting in my bedroom, and now I have just the hardwood floor. We put window shades up instead of curtains, and we put my mattress and pillow in special covers. I also had to get a closed bookcase because the doctor said books collect dust. I even had to take all the pictures off the wall in my room because they collect dust too.

School is a problem because there are so many places dust can accumulate. The only thing I can do is take my medication regularly and try to prevent an episode. So far, everything is working out okay. I haven't had an episode since my diagnosis.

Asthma is a lung disease. It involves chronic inflammation of the airway passages, or bronchi, which carry air into and out of the lungs. Asthma can begin at any age, and it tends to run in families. There is no cure for asthma, but medication helps to control the

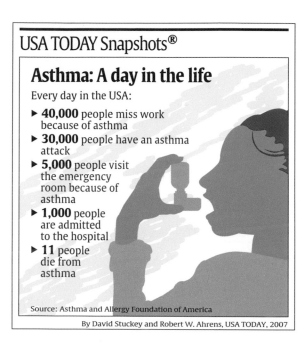

USA TODAY Snapshots®

Asthma: A day in the life

Every day in the USA:

- ▶ **40,000** people miss work because of asthma
- ▶ **30,000** people have an asthma attack
- ▶ **5,000** people visit the emergency room because of asthma
- ▶ **1,000** people are admitted to the hospital
- ▶ **11** people die from asthma

Source: Asthma and Allergy Foundation of America

By David Stuckey and Robert W. Ahrens, USA TODAY, 2007

condition by reducing the inflammation and swelling that cause the airways to become narrower. Asthma sometimes can cause death.

Among children, asthma accounts for more hospitalizations and missed days of school than any other childhood disease. Among adults, it causes many to miss work. More than 20 million Americans have asthma, and 7 million of them are children and young people under the age of eighteen. And the asthma rate is rising. Doctors believe that air pollution is a major factor. Both outdoors and indoors, contaminants fill the air we breathe. Smoke and fumes from factories, as well as motor-vehicle exhaust and building materials irritate our eyes, noses, and lungs. The same is true for household aerosol sprays and cigarette smoke. All of these aggravate the bronchial irritation experienced by people with asthma.

WHAT CAUSES ASTHMA?

Scientists do not fully understand the basic causes of asthma. But doctors do know that there is an abnormality in the lungs of people with asthma that causes the lining of airways to be swollen and tender all the time. This chronic inflammation leaves the airways overly sensitive to changes in the environment. The environmental changes are called triggers. In an asthma episode, the muscle around the airways tightens. Mucus is produced, and the lining of the airways swells even further. The symptoms include wheezing, coughing, shortness of breath, and tightness in the chest.

Asthma triggers include the following:

- infections, such as colds and bronchitis
- lung irritants, such as smoke and fumes from paint or cleaning fluids
- aspirin and other nonsteroidal, anti-inflammatory drugs
- weather conditions, such as cold air and dry wind
- overexertion, such as running too fast or climbing too many stairs
- emotional outbursts, such as becoming very angry or crying or laughing
- allergies, such as to pollen, mold, dust and dust mites, cockroaches, animal dander, and sometimes food

WHAT HAPPENS DURING AN ASTHMA EPISODE?

When an episode occurs and the airways become clogged, it is much harder for the person to breathe in. In addition, excess mucus makes it difficult to exhale. The air stays trapped in the lungs. To get an idea of what it feels like for someone with asthma to try to exhale stale air from the lungs, hold your finger halfway across the hole on one end of a straw and then try to blow a breath of air through the other end. Imagine what it would be like to try to exhale many breaths this way.

During an asthma episode, or attack, breathing becomes more and more difficult. Often the lungs actually hurt. This is similar to

the feeling you get when you take deep breaths of cold air on a wintry day. Air that is exhaled makes a whistling sound as it moves through the narrow airways. Coughing begins, and the plugs of mucus that clog the bronchi often are brought up with the cough. These look like little pieces of string and are called sputum. Asthma attacks can be mild, moderate, or severe. They can last for a few minutes or for days. They can also happen at night. During sleep, the airways become narrow and collect mucus, making breathing more difficult.

ALLERGIC ASTHMA

Allergies sometimes trigger an asthma attack. In allergic asthma, allergens such as pollens, mold spores, dust mites, cockroaches, animal dander, and sometimes food attach to IgE antibodies on sensitized mast cells and basophils. This activates these cells to release histamine and other chemical mediators, which then react in the lungs. They cause the muscle around the airways to tighten, more mucus to be produced, and the lining of the airways to swell. The result is the onset of asthma symptoms— wheezing, coughing, shortness of breath, and tightness in the chest.

Remember that the airways of people with asthma are always inflamed. It is easy, therefore, to understand how coming into contact with an allergen could cause trouble. Imagine having a sore throat and eating a hard pretzel or a piece of dry toast. Swallowing these foods would cause further irritation in your throat. The airways of the lungs of someone with asthma are sore and tender. The exposure to the allergen causes further irritation to the airways, just as the pretzel or the toast causes further irritation to someone with a sore throat.

www.usatoday.com
USA TODAY
News
SECTION A

August 20, 2010

From the Pages of USA TODAY

Household chemicals linked to kids' asthma

The chemical compounds that keep our leftovers fresh and make our floors easy to clean may be a factor in the rising levels of asthma and allergies in children around the world over the past 30 years.

Five million U.S. children have asthma and 10% to 20% of infants have eczema, the Asthma and Allergy Foundation of America reports. The Centers for Disease Control and Prevention estimates the cost of treating asthma in these children at $3.2 billion per year.

An extensive study of Swedish children found that house dust containing the softeners in plastic that give flexibility to food containers, vinyl floor tiles and cling wrap is associated with higher rates of asthma, eczema and other allergy symptoms.

The compounds, phthalates, are widely used in moisturizers, nail polish, insect repellants, shower curtains, hairsprays and building products such as polyvinyl chloride flooring.

Because they leach [seep] out of products, they are considered environmental contaminants. Global phthalate production is 3.8 million tons [3.5 million metric tons] per year. "We've measured lots of things and there are no other factors that have

shown this kind of raised risk," says Carl-Gustaf Bornehag of the Swedish National Testing and Research Institute, lead study author.

The study was published in the October edition of *Environmental Health Perspectives*.

While Bornehag says the research doesn't contain enough evidence "to make us recommend that parents throw out everything that's plastic in their home," he called for serious and rapid research to confirm the findings.

The American Chemistry Council notes that it's hard to tell whether phthalates are the cause of the children's asthma, or an effect.

"It is common practice to replace carpeting with smooth, easy-to-clean surfaces, such as vinyl, in the homes of children suffering from asthma, in order to reduce dust," the council's Marian Stanley says. "So the question is, do the children have asthma because of the vinyl on the floor, or is there vinyl on the floor because they have asthma?"

—Elizabeth Weise

DIAGNOSIS

Pulmonologists are doctors who specialize in lung disease. They can diagnose asthma and help their patients to manage symptoms. Those with allergic asthma should also see an allergist.

To diagnose asthma, the doctor will begin with a detailed patient history. You may be asked:

- What kinds of symptoms are you experiencing? Do you cough or wheeze? Do you have tightness in your chest? Is your nose constantly stuffy or runny? Do you have skin rashes?
- Are your symptoms worse at a certain time of the year? Are your symptoms worse in certain locations, such as at home, at school, or at work? Do your symptoms seem to be worse outdoors or indoors?
- What seems to aggravate your symptoms?
- Do you use medications to treat your symptoms? Which ones seem to help?
- Does anyone in your family have a history of asthma or allergies?

Next, the doctor will watch the way your chest and body posture look when you breathe and will listen for a wheezing sound. The doctor will look for signs of allergies, such as skin rashes and increased mucus production in your nose. If the doctor suspects asthma, tests will confirm the diagnosis. A chest X-ray can help rule out other lung conditions.

A pulmonary function test, or spirometry, involves inhaling and exhaling through a tube attached to a recording machine, called a spirometer. The spirometer registers and graphs your level of respiratory function, or how much air you are able to move in and out of your lungs and how quickly you can do so. The test is done once before you take medication and then again after you have taken it. The medication used during the test is an inhaled drug called a beta-agonist, or bronchodilator, which can quickly open up inflamed airways. It is used by people with asthma when they feel an attack starting. The pulmonary function test confirms a diagnosis of asthma if it shows that your breathing function improves after you take the bronchodilator drug.

Another test, called peak flow monitoring, also can give the doctor valuable information. A device called a peak flow meter measures the amount of air you exhale and the length of time it takes you to do so. This is done twice a day, once in the morning and once in the afternoon. You write down the number the peak flow meter shows each time. Lung function in someone with asthma is usually worse in the morning and better in the afternoon. If the peak flow readings show this pattern, the doctor can confirm that you have asthma.

Then the doctor will do more tests to identify the trigger. Skin and blood tests can determine the source of allergic asthma. The doctor may use an elimination diet if he or she suspects a food allergy. A test of nasal mucus checks for eosinophil cells. Sputum can also be analyzed this way.

A young girl breathes into a peak flow meter. She exhales forcefully into the tube, which measures lung function. Peak flow meters can help determine when to seek emergency medical care, the effectiveness of a person's asthma management and treatment plan, and what triggers an asthma attack.

USA TODAY
HEALTH REPORTS:
DISEASES AND DISORDERS

TREATMENT

There is no cure for asthma. Yet preventive measures can help people cope with the condition.

AVOID THE TRIGGER

In allergic asthma, you must avoid the allergen. (See Chapter 3 on allergic rhinitis for things you can do to avoid airborne allergens.) When avoidance is difficult, your doctor may recommend allergy shots. If a food allergy triggers your asthma, avoid eating the food.

USE THE PROPER MEDICATIONS

Medications can help you stay symptom-free. They reduce the inflammation and swelling that cause the airways to become narrower. Many different medications are available to treat asthma. Because asthma varies from person to person, the type of medication and amounts prescribed vary from person to person. The doctor considers how often the episodes occur and how severe the symptoms are. The doctor then creates a treatment plan that may include a single medication or a combination of a few.

Medications for asthma fall into two groups. One group provides long-term control of the condition. The other gives quick relief of symptoms. The medications for long-term control reduce inflammation and swelling in the airways and prevent symptoms from starting.

The medications provide quick relief and relax and open the airways during an asthma attack. These drugs generally last about four hours. They do not keep symptoms from coming back.

USE A METERED-DOSE INHALER

Medications can be effective only if you use them properly, especially those prescribed for long-term control. Metered-dose inhalers can help. These pocket-size, handheld canisters are designed to send

To treat asthma, doctors often prescribe metered-dose inhalers that deliver medicine to the lungs. These medicines open up constricted airways and can prevent asthma attacks triggered by exercise or cold air.

medication directly to the lungs by way of the mouth. You must hold the inhaler at the proper distance from your mouth. A small tube, called a spacer, can be attached to the inhaler to make this easier. Then you pump the medication into your mouth, inhale it slowly, and hold your breath for a few seconds. Your doctor will instruct you on this the first time you use an inhaler. Using it incorrectly can result in an incorrect dosage, and the medication might not be effective.

USE A PEAK FLOW METER

One of the signs of an approaching asthma attack is difficulty pushing air out of the lungs. A peak flow meter can help determine if an asthma attack is coming on. A drop in peak flow may be a warning. This gives you a chance to take your quick-relief medications before symptoms begin. A peak flow meter also helps you to monitor how well your medications are working and whether the treatment program set up for you is effective. Your doctor will determine your "personal best" peak flow rate. This is what you can strive for to control your asthma.

CONFIRM THAT YOUR MEDICATION IS WORKING

Signs that your asthma medications are working include the following:

- Symptoms of coughing or difficulty breathing rarely or never occur.
- You are able to participate in normal physical activity, including exercise.
- You feel comfortable with your medications and experience no side effects or few side effects.
- Your pulmonary function tests show near-normal breathing.

If you feel that your medications do not relieve your symptoms or cause uncomfortable side effects, tell your doctor right away. Your doctor may have to adjust the medications. Be sure to let the doctor make the decision. Do not change the amount of medication yourself.

TAKING CONTROL OF YOUR ASTHMA

Preventing episodes is the key to controlling asthma. Here are some suggestions that can help:

- Learn to properly use an asthma inhaler and a peak flow meter. Be responsible for taking your medications exactly as your doctor prescribes.
- Know the side effects of the medications you take so that you will be aware of them if they develop.
- Take your medications even when you feel well.
- Keep your doctor's phone number handy.
- Recognize signs that your asthma is getting out of control. Take the appropriate medications to prevent an episode from starting. Call your doctor if necessary.
- Do not use medications other than your asthma medications without first checking with your doctor.

- Take care of your overall health by eating a balanced diet, getting enough sleep, exercising regularly, and reducing stress.
- Avoid air pollution and other lung irritants, such as cigarette smoke and fumes from hair spray, perfume, cologne, paint, and glue.
- Do warm-up exercises before any intense activity.

ASTHMA AND EXERCISE

Avoiding your asthma triggers and closely following your doctor's instructions on taking medications should allow you to participate in most activities, including sports. In fact, exercise should be a part of your daily routine. Aerobic exercise, especially swimming, actually improves the ability of your muscles to use oxygen efficiently. This, in turn, helps you to become a more efficient breather. Your breathing will become easier, even during exertion. And if an asthma episode does arise, you will be better able to manage the symptoms. Other types of exercise that are beneficial include bicycling, weight lifting, and even dance, such as ballet and jazz.

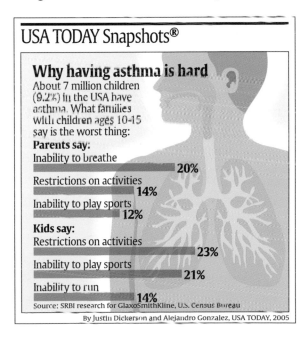

USA TODAY Snapshots®

Why having asthma is hard

About 7 million children (9.2%) in the USA have asthma. What families with children ages 10-15 say is the worst thing:

Parents say:
Inability to breathe — 20%

Restrictions on activities — 14%

Inability to play sports — 12%

Kids say:
Restrictions on activities — 23%

Inability to play sports — 21%

Inability to run — 14%

Source: SRBI research for GlaxoSmithKline, U.S. Census Bureau

By Justin Dickerson and Alejandro Gonzalez, USA TODAY, 2005

CHAPTER NINE

LIVING WITH ALLERGIES

The key to successfully living with allergies is to know as much as possible about them and to work together with family and friends to manage them. Allergies can affect your entire family. Even if just one member of the family has allergies, that person can have an impact on every other member. And friendships can be affected too.

PARENTS

Parents experience a wide range of emotions when they learn that one of their children has allergies. Some parents may be hesitant to use discipline for fear of adding problems to the ones the child already faces. Others feel guilty about giving extra attention to a child with allergies. Some may resent having to change their homes, vacations, or meals to accommodate a child with allergies. And it is not unusual for parents of young people who have had severe allergic reactions or severe asthma episodes to live with a haunting fear that the child will suddenly die. These emotions often create tension within the family.

"Ever since Aaron was stung by the wasp, things haven't been quite the same," says Aaron's mother. "During the warm months, I feel fearful every time he sets foot out of the house. I'm always so worried that he'll be stung and not have his epinephrine with him. He gets very angry when I ask him if he has remembered to take it with him when he leaves the house, but I keep imagining how horrible it would be if he were stung and then didn't have his epinephrine on hand. Who knows, maybe help wouldn't get there in time. It's an awful burden."

SIBLINGS

If you have a brother or sister with allergies, have you ever felt jealous of the attention or special treatment he or she gets from your mom or dad? If you are the one who has allergies, has your brother or sister ever expressed anger or resentment over the attention or special treatment you get from your parents? Allergies cause sibling rivalry in some families. But other families pull together. That is what happened in Paul's family.

"Once we found out I'm allergic to walnuts, my family seemed to get closer," says Paul. "My older brother changed a lot after I was diagnosed. He never seemed to pay much attention to what I was doing before, but once we found out about the allergy, he started to watch over what I ate and made sure I always read the labels on food. Most of the time, he would read the labels along with me, just to make sure. I don't think he totally trusted me to read thoroughly." Then Paul added, "He's away at college now, but when he comes home for the holidays or the summer, he starts right in on checking up on me. I think it's pretty funny, but I like it. It makes me feel like he really cares about me."

The key to successfully living with allergies is to know as much as possible about them and to work together with family and friends to manage them. Even if just one member of a family has allergies, the need for that person to avoid allergens and, in the worst cases, the constant risk of anaphylactic shock can affect the daily lives of every other member. Friends and classmates might not always be supportive because they don't understand the seriousness of the condition. But by working with your doctor to come up with an effective treatment plan, making appropriate lifestyle choices, and educating those around you, you can manage your allergy and live a full and active life.

January 7, 2010

From the Pages of USA TODAY

Food allergy sufferers find socializing tricky

Woe to the waiter who gets Aaron and Kendra Johnson at his table. When the two place an order, questions fly as if it's an episode of *Law & Order*.

Both have severe food allergies, and before they eat any meal outside their home, they typically grill their server about the exact ingredients in a dish, down to what's on the label of a jar of herbs used. They also ask for step-by-step details about how it's been prepared.

When the couple recently went out for dinner in Seattle, Aaron says, "we got a deer-in-the-headlights look from the waitress. Sometimes a server can get put off, too."

What makes a meal out even more complicated for the pair is that their allergies are not to the same foods. Aaron, 29, was diagnosed with a life-threatening cow's milk allergy when he was 12. Kendra, 31, breaks out in hives and can have swallowing and breathing difficulties if she eats gluten, a protein found in wheat, oat, barley and rye.

For the Johnsons and anyone else with food allergies or some other food limitations, dining out, eating in other people's homes, and munching at office parties and school events can be a minefield. One bite of the wrong cupcake or cookie and a person could face days of illness, lost work or worse—anaphylactic shock.

Experts believe a growing number of Americans have food-related illnesses, says Calman Prussin, an immunologist with the National Institute of Allergy and Infectious Diseases. Though the illnesses appear to be increasing, the trend may partly be the result of increased awareness and testing.

Phadia US, the largest allergy blood test maker in the world, has grown from testing about 10,000 patients in 2002 to about 1 million this year, says physician Robert Reinhardt, senior director of medical, regulatory and quality at Phadia.

Though more allergy-safe edibles can be found on grocery shelves and more restaurants are becoming sensitive to special diet needs, many people with food allergies say staying healthy is not as easy as simply asking for a "wheat-free" or "nut-free" (or whatever your poison is) dish.

Hostesses get hurt feelings, well-meaning friends and relatives make food-preparation mistakes, and waiters and chefs can be surly or misunderstand instructions, the Johnsons say. Other food preparers just don't care or don't have time, they say. For some on restricted diets, sometimes it's just easier to stay home and cook for yourself, says Charlotte Riggs, 23, a lab assistant at the University of California-Berkeley who has peanut allergies.

"Having food allergies can be socially isolating," Prussin says.

David Sarwer, director of the Stunkard Weight Management Program at the University of Pennsylvania, says some people who live with allergies, especially those who have had life-threatening experiences, can harbor food fears that verge on eating-disorder behavior.

"I've had patients who've literally said they'd rather die than use an EpiPen because it's so embarrassing," Prussin says. "And I wonder: Where did they get that message?"

Coping strategies

Eight types of food account for 90% of all food-allergic reactions in the USA: milk, eggs, peanuts, tree nuts (such as walnuts, almonds, cashews, pecans), wheat, soy, fish and shellfish, according to Centers for Disease Control and Prevention [CDC] statistics.

Food allergy reactions can happen within seconds to hours after a tainted dish has been tasted and can affect the body numerous ways, says Karl von Tiehl, assistant clinical professor at Cincinnati Children's Medical Center Division of Allergy & Immunology. Reactions include breaking out in hives, eczema, vomiting, diarrhea, bloating and gas.

According to the National Institute of Allergy and Infectious Diseases, food allergies cause 30,000 cases of anaphylaxis, 2,000 hospitalizations and 150 deaths each year. But a more recent 2009 report from the CDC indicates as many as 9,500 children are hospitalized due to food allergies.

One of the greatest hurdles to a person with food issues, especially to common foods, is how to negotiate a normal social life in a food-centric world, says Robert Wood, director of pediatric allergy and immunology at Johns Hopkins Children's Center in Baltimore [Maryland].

Elisabeth Hasselbeck, co-host of *The View*, says she has developed coping strategies since her diagnosis of celiac disease 10 years ago. Author of *The G-Free Diet, a Gluten-free Survival Guide*, Hasselbeck says the day before arriving at a restaurant, she calls to ask about gluten-free options.

"Talk to a manager. Get as high up on the chain as possible, and then ask again when you get to the restaurant. The more emphatic and nice you are, the better. Literally, don't bite the hand that feeds you," Hasselbeck says.

Allergic diners should never get too comfy, though. "Ordering in restaurants is fraught with peril," von Tiehl says. A utensil used in multiple bowls, residue left on pots and cutting boards, even chef's hands can transfer allergens among dishes.

[see page 110 for the rest of the article]

Plan ahead for travel

Even restaurants that claim to be allergy-aware are fallible. "We went out to dinner at a place we'd eaten before and they'd switched the vendor for one food, but I didn't realize it. I got home and had a terrible time breathing and spent two hours on the bathroom floor," Aaron Johnson says.

But when there are no food options— say, friends spontaneously want to go out— sometimes the solution is simply skipping the meal and grabbing a bite later, Kendra Johnson says. "Our friends like this brewery, and Aaron likes beer, and I don't want to deny him that. So sometimes, I just go without and enjoy the social aspect."

Even family members don't always comprehend the seriousness of food-related illnesses.

Marty Guenther, 57, from Rochester, N.Y., who was recently diagnosed with celiac disease, says, "My sister once said to me, 'Why do you want everybody to be miserable like you?'"

Guenther brings her own food to gatherings to avoid long conversations with her hosts about what they're serving. Charlotte Riggs, the UC lab assistant, says her college, Wesleyan, was accommodating after she had a serious reaction in the cafeteria to bread that contained tree nuts. "I arranged some meetings. I interviewed all the dining hall managers at all of the facilities on campus. Within a couple weeks, they had signs on everything that contained peanuts," Riggs says.

Traveling can be hairy as well, but staying in digs with a kitchen where you can make your own meals, mailing your own food ahead to a hotel, and picking vacation locales with Whole Foods, Wegmans and other grocery chains that carry a plethora of allergen-free options smooth the way, say allergy sufferers.

Guenther found a haven at Disney World. "They made Mickey Mouse-shaped waffles on a gluten-free waffle iron. My gosh, that was one of the highlights of my trip," she says. Some baseball teams, like the Washington Nationals, now offer peanut-free sections at some games.

Penn's Sarwer says food allergy patients may gain comfort realizing "they're not alone in the boat." He says, "The reality of eating in America today, because of obesity and diabetes problems, is that we all have to be diligent and thoughtful about what we eat at every single meal."

Prussin says sticking to a restricted diet and carrying an EpiPen if you're anaphylactic are the best peace-of-mind strategies. And though a cure may be a ways off, he says new management options are around the corner. Scientists are developing novel diagnostic and immunotherapeutic approaches and finding successes in test groups, he says.

Meanwhile, the Johnsons are thankful for their understanding friends and family and are determined not to cloister themselves at home out of self-consciousness. And trying not to rock the boat at a social occasion and swallowing an unknown morsel just isn't worth putting your health and life in jeopardy, Kendra says.

—*Mary Brophy Marcus*

FRIENDS

Not everyone believes that allergies are real. People who have never experienced an allergic reaction sometimes have a hard time believing that taking an antibiotic can cause hives and swelling or that eating a morsel of a peanut can cause shortness of breath and loss of consciousness. And some people have trouble understanding how something invisible, such as dust mites, can cause severe breathing problems for people with asthma.

"When I would go to the nurse's office to take my asthma medication, some of the girls in school used to accuse me of trying to get out of class," says Melissa. "They didn't believe that I really needed it. In fact, one of them even said she thought I was faking my asthma symptoms. It really hurt my feelings."

Have your friends ever said, "You're just trying to get attention," or "You're making a big deal out of nothing"? Many people lack information about what allergies are. They think you're exaggerating or overreacting when you avoid being around animals or eating a certain food. The solution is to help your friends learn more about allergies.

ALLERGIES AND SCHOOL

At school the air you breathe is filled with allergens, and their presence can cause problems for you if you have allergies or allergic asthma. Although you do not have control over the school environment, you do have control over your treatment. Your teachers, school administrators, and the school nurse should provide a place for you to take your medications and should allow time for you to do so. When your symptoms flare up or cause you an unusual amount of discomfort, these people also should be willing to excuse your absence from school. Your job, in return, is to avoid your allergen whenever possible and follow your doctor's instructions.

www.usatoday.com

USA TODAY

News

SECTION A

March 7, 2007

From the Pages of USA TODAY

Allergies and asthma don't have to sideline young athletes; Precautions keep them in the game

Brant has had allergies and asthma since he was a toddler. He has been hospitalized numerous times. But the California teen hasn't let it stop him from becoming a top athlete. "He's a freshman in high school, and he's the starting catcher for the varsity team this spring," says his mother, Lisa.

Several decades ago, it was inconceivable that an athlete with asthma could perform competitively. But experts say there is no reason a person with allergies or asthma cannot reach any level of competition he wishes. "Proper diagnosis, sticking with a medication regime, premedicating and taking precautions are the key," says Kenneth Rundell, a professor of health science at the Center for Healthy Families at Marywood University in Scranton, Pa.

The American Academy of Allergy Asthma and Immunology estimates that 35.9 million Americans have seasonal allergies. Marshall Plaut, chief of the allergic mechanisms section at the National Institute of Allergy and Infectious Diseases, adds that asthma is relatively common among allergy sufferers.

Because oxygen intake increases during exercise, athletes with seasonal allergies may experience symptoms when exposed to airborne allergens, experts say. "When respiration is up, you're going to get a much higher load. Factors like how sensitive you are, pollen count and if you are appropriately medicated are huge," Rundell says.

Alisa Harvey, 41, an elite masters runner from Manassas, Va., has had allergies since her 20s but did not visit an allergist until her 30s. "He did a skin test, and I learned exactly what I am allergic to," she says, noting that trees, grass, ragweed, dust and pets bring on her symptoms.

To persevere, she says, "you just have to be creative about how you go about training and competing." The world record holder for her age group in the indoor women's mile, she has found that ocean-side races are less pollen-heavy, for example.

Exercisers need to be body-aware, Rundell says. When Brant Whiting's breathing becomes labored during team runs, he switches to push-ups and sit-ups, which do not tax his respiratory system as heavily.

With planning and care, people with asthma can enjoy participating in athletic activities.

asthma, he may require prescription nasal steroids, "controller" medications such as inhaled corticosteroids, allergists say.

Allergy desensitization shots and newer steroid drugs also are options to discuss with an allergist.

And if you can't catch a breath and have to hang up your sneakers 15 minutes early one day, don't sweat it, Lisa Whiting says: "It isn't going to make a whole lot of difference in the long run."

—*Mary Brophy Marcus*

His mother says she always has a talk with his coaches before each season, teaching them about body postures and breathing sounds that may indicate Brant is verging on an attack. She also encourages Brant to trust his instincts about how he feels, even if a coach is pushing him.

Medications for athletes may include over-the-counter antihistamines. But if a person has more severe allergies and

ALLERGIES AND TRAVEL

When your family plans a vacation or your teacher arranges a field trip, plan ahead. If you have food allergies, decide how you are going to avoid the offending foods. You may have to pack food from home. If you are allergic to pollens, plan to travel in an air-conditioned car or bus, if possible, so that the windows are closed. If you are allergic to dust and dust mites, you may have to carry nonallergenic mattress and pillow covers to use in hotel rooms. Some hotels allow pets in the rooms. So if you are allergic to animal dander, be prepared to stay in a room that may be filled with your allergen. Take along the medications that will help you prevent symptoms from starting.

Seasonal vacation places, such as summer cabins or motels, tend to be especially prone to mold growth because they are closed up for several months of the year. If you are allergic to molds, try not to stay in these buildings at the beginning of the summer season. Try to stay in them later in the season, after they have been ventilated for a while.

TAKING CONTROL OF YOUR ALLERGIES

Educating yourself and being prepared are the two most important things you can do to cope with your allergies. Other strategies include the following:

- Avoid your allergen and take your medications exactly as your doctor prescribes. If you are supposed to carry injectable epinephrine, take it with you when you leave the house. Be certain that you know how to use it.
- Make it your responsibility to avoid your allergen and to remember to take your medications. Do not rely on other people to remind you.
- Think ahead and anticipate times when you could be at risk for

having an allergic reaction. Either avoid the situation or take measures to ensure your safety.

- Never take chances. Do not eat even a small amount of a food you know you are supposed to avoid. Do not take a medication that you know has caused even a slight reaction in the past.
- If there is an activity that you want to do that puts your safety at risk, choose an alternate activity. For example, if you want to play a sport and you are allergic to bee venom, choose an indoor sport, such as basketball, over an outdoor sport, such as baseball or soccer.
- Pursue interests that help you feel good about yourself. Self-confidence will help you get through the times when coping with your allergies may be difficult.

Research is ongoing in the field of allergies. Scientists constantly search for new and better ways to manage allergies. Some even believe that an allergy vaccine is on the horizon—one that would prevent allergies from developing in the first place.

GLOSSARY

allergen: a substance that causes an allergic reaction

allergic rhinitis: an allergy to pollens, mold spores, dust mites, cockroaches, or animal dander that causes inflammation of the nose

allergist: a doctor who specializes in treating allergic conditions, including asthma triggered by allergy

allergy: an abnormal response by the immune system to a substance that does not cause a reaction in most people

anaphylaxis: a potentially fatal allergic reaction that affects the entire body. Symptoms may include hives, difficulty in breathing, and a drop in blood pressure.

angioedema: swelling of various body parts, especially around the eyes and lips

animal dander: flaky cells that animals and birds shed from their skin, fur, and feathers

antibody: a serum protein that fights infection or causes allergy

antihistamine: a drug commonly used to treat the symptoms of allergy. The drug blocks histamine and relieves symptoms.

asthma: a lung disease characterized by chronic inflammation of the airways

asthma episode: a worsening of asthma symptoms that can be life threatening and is sudden, severe, or both; also called an asthma attack

atopic dermatitis: a dry, itchy skin rash that can occur after exposure to an allergen; also called eczema

basophils: white blood cells that contain many kinds of chemical mediators

bronchi: the main airways of the lungs

bronchodilator: a drug that relieves the tightening of the muscle surrounding the airways

chemical mediators: chemicals, such as histamine, contained in mast cells and basophils

chronic inflammation: the constant swelling and tenderness of the airways of people who have asthma

corticosteroids: drugs used to reduce inflammation in the lungs or nasal passages

cromolyn sodium: a drug used to reduce inflammation during allergic rhinitis and asthma episodes

decongestant: a drug used to relieve mucus congestion in the nose or nasal passages

eczema: a dry, itchy skin rash that can be caused by allergies; also called atopic dermatitis

eosinophils: white blood cells involved in allergic reactions; also known as allergy cells

epinephrine: a hormonelike drug that can reverse an anaphylactic reaction

food allergy: an allergic reaction to a food, involving IgE antibodies

hay fever: seasonal allergy to pollens and molds

histamine: a chemical released by mast cells and basophils that causes itching, swelling, and inflammation during allergic reactions

hives: itchy red bumps on the skin that can be caused by an allergic reaction; also called wheals

immune system: the body system, made up of the bone marrow, thymus gland, and lymph nodes, that protects against disease and infections

immunotherapy: specific desensitization, or allergy shots, used for allergies to pollen, mold, dust mite, animal dander, and insect venom

inflammation: swelling and tissue damage in the body that occurs when cells gather and release chemical mediators in response to foreign substances or injury

lymphocytes: white blood cells manufactured in bone marrow; an important part of the immune system

mast cells: cells containing histamine and other chemical mediators that are found in the mucous membranes, bronchial tubes, and skin

metered-dose inhaler: a pocket-size canister with a mouthpiece that contains asthma medications that are inhaled

mold spores: the tiny seeds released by molds during reproduction

mucus: a fluid produced by glands in the body. Mucus cleans and protects membranes that line cavities exposed to the environment, such as nostrils.

peak flow meter: a small handheld device that a person breaths into to monitor the rate of air flow from the lungs

pollen: tiny grains released from trees, grasses, weeds, and flowers during reproduction

pulmonologist: a doctor who specializes in treating lung diseases, such as asthma

sensitization: the process by which people with a tendency toward developing allergies are repeatedly exposed to allergens and then develop allergies

sinusitis: inflammation of the sinuses

spirometer: a machine into which a person breathes in order to determine his or her level of respiratory function. The machine records and graphs the information, which shows how much air can be moved in and out of the lungs and how quickly this can be done.

steroids: hormones, such as cortisone, that regulate body functions and are produced by the body's endocrine glands; used in some allergy and asthma medications

topical medication: medication that is applied to the skin

urticaria: small red bumps on the skin that can be caused by allergies; also called hives or wheals

wheal: a small red bump on the skin that can be caused by allergies; also called urticaria or hives

RESOURCES

American Academy of Allergy, Asthma and Immunology (AAAAI)
555 East Wells Street, Suite 1100
Milwaukee, WI 53202-3823
(414) 272-6071
http://www.aaaai.org

This nonprofit medical specialty association represents allergists and other doctors and health professionals with special interest in allergy. The AAAAI's mission is to advance knowledge and communicate information about allergy, asthma, and immunology.

American College of Allergy, Asthma and Immunology (ACAAI)
85 West Algonquin Road
Suite 550
Arlington Heights, IL 60005-4425
(847) 427-1200
http://www.acaai.org

This organization provides information on allergies and asthma to increase public awareness and to educate people about these conditions. The website provides a list of allergists in your area.

American Lung Association
61 Broadway, 6th Floor
New York, NY 10006
(800-LUNG-USA), or (800-586-4872)
http://www.lungusa.org

The American Lung Association has offices around the country that provide information about asthma education programs; asthma camps; support groups; and resources for children, parents, teachers, and health professionals.

Asthma and Allergy Foundation of America
1233 20th Street NW
Suite 402
Washington, DC 20036
(202) 466-7643, or (800-7-ASTHMA)
http://www.aafa.org

This organization is dedicated to educating people about asthma and allergies and helping those who have these conditions. It has a nationwide network of regional chapters and educational support groups. Included are support groups solely for teens with asthma.

Food Allergy & Anaphylaxis Network
11781 Lee Jackson Highway, Suite 160
Fairfax, VA 22033
(800) 929-4040
http://www.foodallergy.org

The Food Allergy Network provides information for young people, parents, and teachers about coping with food allergies.

MedicAlert Foundation
2323 Colorado Avenue
Turlock, CA 95382
(888) 633-4298
http://www.medicalert.org

MedicAlert is a nonprofit organization that has been endorsed by leading medical associations across the nation. It was founded by a physician and his wife. MedicAlert medical emergency bracelets and necklaces can be purchased through this organization.

Pollen.com
220 West Germantown Pike
Plymouth Meeting, PA 19462
(610) 834-0800
http://www.pollen.com

This website was created by SDI Health, an organization that collects data on illness and condition trends across the United States. Pollen.com provides allergy information and weather forecasts that hay fever sufferers can use to help manage their symptoms.

U.S. Environmental Protection Agency
Ariel Rios Building
1200 Pennsylvania Avenue NW
Washington, DC 20460
(202) 272-0167
http://www.epa.gov

The Environmental Protection Agency, a federal organization concerned with toxins and hazardous materials, provides information about air-filtering devices that can be used in your home.

SELECTED BIBLIOGRAPHY

Corren, Jonathan. *100 Questions and Answers about Allergies*. Sudbury, MA: Jones and Bartlett, 2010.

Mahmoudi, Massoud. *Allergy and Asthma: Practical Diagnosis and Management*. New York: McGraw-Hill, 2007.

Naff, Clayton F. *Allergies*. Farmington Hills, MI: Greenhaven, 2010.

FURTHER READING AND WEBSITES

Books

Berger, William E. *Teen's Guide to Living with Asthma*. New York: Facts On File, 2007.

Bock, Kenneth, and Cameron Stauth. *Healing the New Childhood Epidemics: Autism, ADHD, Asthma, and Allergies*. Chicago: Ballantine Books, 2008.

Bruce-Gardyne, Lucinda. *Food Allergy Cookbook*. New York: Reader's Digest, 2008.

Brynie, Faith Hickman. *101 Questions about Your Immune System*. Minneapolis: Twenty-First Century Books, 2000.

Hyde, Margaret O., and Elizabeth Forsyth, MD. *Stress 101: An Overview for Teens*. Minneapolis: Twenty-First Cewntury Books, 2008.

Miller, Sloane. *Allergic Girl: Adventures in Living Well with Food Allergies*. Hoboken, NJ: Wiley, 2011.

Murphy, Wendy. *Asthma*. Minneapolis: Twenty-First Century Books, 2011.

Websites

Mayo Clinic
http://www.mayoclinic.com/health/asthma/DS00021

The renowned Mayo Clinic provides an in-depth look at the causes, symptoms, and treatment of asthma.

Medline Plus
http://www.nlm.nih.gov/medlineplus/

MedlinePlus is the National Institutes of Health's website for patients and their families and friends. The site provides information about diseases, conditions, and wellness issues in simple, straightforward language. For information on allergies, go to http://www.nlm.nih.gov/medlineplus/allergy.html.

National Institute of Allergy and Infectious Diseases
http://www.niaid.nih.gov

The National Institute of Allergy and Infectious Diseases provides information about allergies and infectious diseases, including a comprehensive resource list.

TeensHealth
http://kidshealth.org/teen

TeensHealth is a project of the Nemours Foundation, one of the largest nonprofit organizations devoted to children's health. The site provides information on a wide range of physical, emotional, and behavioral issues that affect children and teens. For information on allergies, go to http://kidshealth.org/teen/diseases_conditions/allergies_immune/allergies.html.

LERNER

SOURCE

Expand learning beyond the printed book. Download free, complementary educational resources for this book from our website, www.lerneresource.com.

INDEX

ABOUT THE AUTHOR

Wendy Moragne is a former teacher who has written on medical topics. She is currently practicing law and lives in Moorestown, New Jersey.

PHOTO ACKNOWLEDGMENTS